Equip & Perfect:

Worship

A 52-Week Devotional for the Worship Team

DR. A. BEN CHERIYAN

WESTBOW
PRESS®
A DIVISION OF THOMAS NELSON
& ZONDERVAN

WestBow Press books may be ordered through booksellers or by contacting:

WestBow Press
A Division of Thomas Nelson & Zondervan
1663 Liberty Drive
Bloomington, IN 47403
www.westbowpress.com
1 (866) 928-1240

ISBN: 978-1-5127-6499-4 (sc)
ISBN: 978-1-5127-6500-7 (e)

Library of Congress Control Number: 2016919426

Print information available on the last page.

WestBow Press rev. date: 11/29/2016

Table of Contents

Outcomes & Effects of Worship

Supplemental Devotionals—
Special Services/ Holy Days

This book is dedicated to my beautiful
wife, daughter and son,
for your love, support, prayers, and patience.

And I give thanks to my Lord and Savior
Jesus Christ, for without Him,
I would not be who am I today.

Preface

As a worship team, we spend a lot of time rehearsing and preparing for the service, which includes vocal and musical arrangements, stage and lighting preparation, audio-visual productions, as well as many additional components necessary for a "smooth" worship service. Things can get hectic, and sometimes we get so caught up in all the details that we can lose sight of why we worship. Spiritually we need to grow together, and it's important that we sit in His presence as a group. We must spend time IN worship before we can lead others TO worship. This includes time in prayer as well. It will allow the teams to align and work together as one cohesive unit as well as allow us to experience an atmosphere of true worship during our services.

Equip & Perfect – Worship is based on Ephesians 4:12 "to equip His people for works of service." The Amplified Bible says "to fully **equip and perfect** the saints for works of service." The purpose of this devotional is to be a resource for the worship team (including all musicians, vocalists, leaders, AV teams and other teams involved) so that they can come together prior to rehearsal or service for a time of teaching, learning, encouraging, strengthening and for a time of prayer. This could be for a few minutes before the service, or one day during the week for any amount of time to discuss the topics and any questions team members may have. These topics have been carefully selected taking into consideration my experiences as a worship leader, choir director, and academic preparation towards a degree in worship.

This book presents a weekly devotional with topics that are relevant for the personal and corporate growth of the worship team. Each devotional will be based on a biblical story, parable, biblical figure, and/ or verse as the main subject, and include contemporary application in worship, as well as in the life of the team member. It may also contain additional reading, references throughout the text, and relevant Christian and Greek terminology (in bold). Reflections at the end of each topic are meant to encourage discussion and dialogue. Each devotional can be a guide for a more in-depth discussion of the topics. The devotion leader can focus on any area in the week's topic that can benefit the group, and he/she can explore further based on the needs of the team. (*Note: The leader should also keep in mind to skip to the special devotionals prepared for Easter and Christmas).

The devotionals are separated into larger categories:

1. **Purpose & Significance of Worship**
2. **Qualities & Characteristics of the Team Member**
3. **Expressions of Worship**
4. **Biblical Influencers of Worship**
5. **Leading in the Spirit**
6. **Styles of Worship**
7. **The Role of the Worship Team**
8. **Outcomes & Effects of Worship**
9. **Special Services/ Holy Days**

I encourage every team member to read each week's devotional (and any additional suggested reading) prior to meeting up with the team. This will give a better understanding on the topic and set the stage for a more robust discussion. These are not only meant as a discussion tool, but to learn biblical truths and real life applications. I pray that as you spend time with each devotional, you learn more about God's will for the team and in your own personal lives, that you grow in Him, and appreciate more and more why He is worthy of all of our heartfelt worship.

Introduction

We serve a wonderful and all-powerful God, the creator of the heavens and the Earth. And as the Son of God, Jesus Christ came down and sacrificed Himself so that we could be made free from the bondage of sin. This alone should be reason enough to offer unencumbered praises and worship to Him. In Psalm 22:3 (NKJV), we see that God delights in our worship and is "enthroned in the praises of Israel." This means that God is fond of our worship.

In the Old Testament worship was costly, with the shedding of blood through sacrifice, a heavy reminder of the cost of sin. King David, however, modified traditional worship and focused it more on the heart. "The sacrifices of God are a broken spirit; a broken and contrite heart" says Psalm 51:17 (NKJV). But Jesus paid the final sacrifice so that no further shedding of blood was needed for the forgiveness of sins. Old covenant prayer and worship was limited to the priests. New covenant prayer and worship is for all who believe that Jesus saved them. "For God so loved the world that he gave his only begotten Son, that whoever believes in Him shall not perish but have everlasting life" John 3:16 (NKJV).

Worship also allows us to freely experience the gifts of the Spirit. We can experience this with corporate worship and also with personal worship. With worship our spirit communicates with the Spirit of God. Through this communion and worship we can also seek God's will and receive direction in our lives.

What is Worship?

1) <u>To Give Thanks</u>

Psalm 100:4–5 says, "Enter his gates with thanksgiving and his courts with praise; give thanks to him and praise his name. For the LORD is good and his love endures forever; his faithfulness continues through all generations." God watches over us and gives us a plan in accordance to His will. Jeremiah 29:11 says, "For I know the plans I have for you," declares the LORD, "plans to prosper you and not to harm you, plans to give you hope and a future." How great is our God that He has a specific plan laid out for our future. How can we not give thanks and worship to such an awesome and loving God?

2) <u>To Celebrate His Goodness and Greatness</u>

Psalm 95:1–7 reads:

1   Come, let us sing for joy to the Lord; let us shout aloud to the Rock of our salvation.

2   Let us come before him with thanksgiving and extol him with music and song.

3   For the Lord is the great God, the great King above all gods.

4   In his hand are the depths of the earth, and the mountain peaks belong to him.

5 The sea is his, for he made it, and his hands formed the dry land.
6 Come, let us bow down in worship, let us kneel before the Lord our Maker;
7 for he is our God and we are the people of his pasture, the flock under his care.

3) To Get Closer to God

James 4:8 says, "Come near to God and He will come near to you." As we spend time in worship and prayer, we grow closer to God. By being in an atmosphere of worship and being open to Him, we can have a better understanding of His purpose and will in our lives.

4) An Environment For God's Dwelling

Worship attracts the presence of the Spirit of God. In Old Testament times, people had to offer burnt offering and sacrifices, and if it was pleasing to God, His presence was in that place. Because of the ultimate sacrifice paid on the cross by Jesus, we no longer have to do this. However, we can still offer up praises and our worship as our sacrifice. Jonah 2:9 says "But, I with shouts of grateful praise, will sacrifice to You."

5) God's Presence

In Revelation chapter 4, the angels and elders are continuously singing praises in His presence. Day and night they never stop saying "Holy, Holy, Holy is the Lord God Almighty, who was and is and is to come" (v.8). And as the angels say this, the twenty-four elders fall before God and worship Him. If heavenly worship is like this, then the worship we give here on Earth is insufficient. However, God looks at the heart; and if the worship we give is genuine and seeking, it will be pleasing to Him, and the Holy Spirit will dwell in our lives.

6) <u>As a Weapon</u>

In Acts chapter 16 we see Paul and Silas praying and singing hymns to God while in jail (especially after being flogged and beaten!) An earthquake shook the ground, the doors to the cells were open, and the prisoners' chains were loosened.

In Joshua 6, the walls of Jericho fell when the Israelites shouted and sounded the trumpets. God's power can come into a place of worship. Satan cannot function in a place where true worship is occurring. If we are constantly worshiping, we cannot submit to any attack of Satan, thereby ensuring that God's will and guidance takes precedence in our lives.

Purpose & Significance of Worship

1

Who Is God and Why Do We Worship Him?

Yours, Lord, is the greatness and the power and the glory and the majesty and the splendor, for everything in heaven and earth is yours. Yours, Lord, is the kingdom; you are exalted as head over all.
1 Chronicles 29:11
Read Psalm 139:1-12

In the first book of the Bible, Genesis, the very first verse says, "In the beginning God". The Bible begins with God. In the very last book of Revelation, the last chapter says, "I am the Alpha and the Omega, the first and the last, the beginning and the end." In the beginning there was God, and in the end there is God. He is infinite. God exists everywhere (omnipresent), knows everything (omniscient), and has all power and authority (omnipotent). This amazing and awesome God created us in His image. The Creator of the universe created us, so that we could be with Him. What an amazing concept. So what can we do? We can offer Him all our praises and worship the almighty Creator.

Worship is communion and communication between God and the worshiper. Psalm 22:3 (NKJV) states, "But you are holy, enthroned in the praises of Israel." God resides amongst His people—us—and our worship is pleasing to Him.

One of the Greek translations of worship, **proskuneo,** means to kiss, crouch to, and pay homage. It is also identified with subjects falling to kiss the ground before a king. When bowing to a king, one can bow down out of respect, or one can truly revel in the king's presence and bow down in awe and adoration. It is in this definition we should regard worship to our Creator, in complete awe and reverence. If this attitude is in our hearts, then the worship and praise that comes out of our hearts and mouths are truly genuine and pure.

We can see many examples in the Bible where God's presence is manifested because worship was occurring. This does not mean that God can only act when there is worship. God is omnipotent and omnipresent. There are, however, specific examples in the Old and New Testaments that demonstrate acts of God during worship.

Words and phrases like acts of praise, adoration, and thankful acknowledgement refer to worship as more of an act or state of mind. It is a time when we worship with an adoring, thankful, and grateful heart. Worship must also be a two-way process, with us giving to God our praise and attention, and then receiving from Him His Word and instruction.

We worship because He loves us. 1 John 4:19 says, "We love because He first loved us." He loved us enough to create us and to dwell among us. And even after sin separated us, He still loved us enough to sacrifice his only Son Jesus. What more reason do we need to worship? We love him because He loves us.

Reflection

❖ How can we worship while we are on stage singing, playing an instrument, or involved in other aspects like sound, lights, or media?

2

Made To Worship

All things have been created through him and for him.
Colossians 1:16
Read Genesis 1 and Psalm 139:13–16

Last week we discussed who God is and why we worship Him. To better understand why we worship, we must recognize who we are. In Genesis 1:26–27 God said, "Let us make mankind in our image, in our likeness…So God created mankind in his own image, in the image of God he created him; male and female he created them." "God saw all that he made, and it was **very** good" (v.31). We are divinely designed by an all-powerful God, and He was pleased when he created us. In Deuteronomy 7:6, He tells us that we are his "treasured possessions." In Ephesians 2:10 (NKJV), Paul tells us "we are God's workmanship." We are God's masterpiece. He has created us anew in Christ Jesus so we can do the good things he planned for us long ago. In Psalm 139:14, he reminds us that we are "fearfully and wonderfully made."

But why did God create humanity? Why not just stop at the Earth and celestial heavens and beings? Or just with the animal kingdom? He created us like Him so that we could have consciousness and choose to commune and have a relationship with Him. God tells us in Isaiah 43:21 that we are "the people I formed for myself." He knew us before we were born. "Before I formed you in the womb I knew you, before you were born I set you apart; I appointed you" (Jeremiah 1:4–5).

So since he created us, was it in vain? Was it only so that we could have great careers, a great family life, and to enjoy our personal lives and accomplishments? God wants us to achieve our best, but that is not our sole purpose. We all have an inner longing within our selves for something of deeper meaning—something spiritual. Unfortunately many people who do not know God try to satisfy this feeling with material things or with emotional and physical pleasures. This is why so many of us are lost today. We continue to hear of celebrities falling into drug and alcohol abuse. We read about millionaires seeking pleasures through infidelity or other avenues. You would think these individuals have it all. But what many are missing is that communion with their Creator—a relationship with God.

When we have true worship, we connect with God in an intimate way. When we acknowledge and focus on Him, the Holy Spirit gives us peace and comfort, no matter what our situation. God is worthy of our worship because He is God, but He also connects to us through worship. And this is God's desire; to be with us as we seek Him. God made you and wants you to be with Him. We are made by Him, and we are made for Him.

<u>Reflection</u>

❖ Do you have an inner longing for a deeper connection with God? Why or Why not?

❖ How can worship help bring you closer to Him?

3

Ministering to the Lord

Give to the Lord the glory due His name; bring
an offering, and come before Him.
Oh, worship the Lord in the beauty of holiness.
1 Chronicles 16:29 (NKJV)
Read Luke 10:38–41

Leitourgeo is the Greek word found in the New Testament, which means to be a public servant or to minister. This is where the word liturgy, the works of the people, comes from. When we minister to the Lord, we offer him all of our worship, all of our words, and all of our works. Ministering to the Lord is the work, actions and words of His people. This does not mean that our actions save us. We are saved because of grace. Once we realize that, all our "works" come out of our adoration and worship to Him.

We must get into the habit of putting God first before we do anything. This may not always be convenient, but there is a deep and revealing truth behind it. In Luke 10:39–40 (NKJV) we see that Mary "sat at Jesus' feet and heard His word. But Martha was distracted with much serving". Martha was anxious over many things, and she wanted to make sure everything was in order. Her sister Mary, however, wanted to hear all that Jesus had to say and put the housework second.

When we go to Him in prayer and worship, we should not just ask for things we want, but we must acknowledge Him first for who He is. There is a story about Abraham Lincoln and an elderly woman that visited him. After making an appointment, she came to see the president. She stated that all she wanted was to bring him a box of cookies, because she knew he enjoyed them so much. Overjoyed he said, "Madam, I thank you for your thoughtful gift. Since I have been President of this country, thousands of people have come into this office asking for favors and demanding things from me. You are the first person who has ever entered these premises asking no favor, and indeed, bring a gift for me."[1] Many times we go to God with our prayers, petitions and requests, but ministering to Him means going to Him in simple adoration and with our praises and worship. "Ministry **to** the Lord leads to ministry **from** the Lord. Ministry to the Lord comes before ministry to man."[2] *(emphasis added)*

Reflection

- ❖ What can we do before, during, and after the worship service to "minister to the Lord"?

4

Corporate vs. Personal Worship

*Every day they continue to meet together in the
temple courts. They broke bread in their homes and
ate together with glad and sincere hearts, praising
God and enjoying the favor of all the people.*
Acts 2:46–47
Read Acts 2:41–47 and Acts 4:32-37

Corporate worship occurs when we worship together with
fellow believers. Personal worship happens when we have
personal devotion on our own time. It is important for both
types of worship to take place in our lives.

Corporate worship is important because the church
is the body of Christ, and we need fellowship with other
Christians in order to grow as one body. It is also important
for our own spiritual growth. We worship together and we
grow together. We can support each other during sorrowful
times, and we can celebrate together during life's victories.
By sharing in similar experiences, we are encouraged and
strengthened by each other. Not being involved in corporate
worship can weaken us during trials and difficult times. In
order for corporate worship to be meaningful, the personal

state of the believer must be in a position of earnestly seeking the will of God.

Personal worship is also vital (we will discuss further in week 14). Personal worship will give us the strength we need to get through our daily lives. It is a time to sit in the presence of God and grow closer to Him. During our personal worship, we should also spend time studying the Word. This quiet time of worship and study allows us to appreciate who God is, while He reminds us to "be still and know that I am God" (Psalm 46:10). A spiritual revelation must take place in the heart of the believer. This occurs only through a personal relationship with God, and it will lead to a more effective spiritual life.

Reflection

❖ What steps can we take to be more involved in corporate worship?

❖ How can you know if your personal worship is effective?

5

Biblical History of Worship

Jesus replied, "Love the Lord your God with all your heart and with all your soul and with all your mind. This is the first and greatest commandment."
Matthew 22:37–38

There are many biblical examples of worship in both the Old and New Testaments. In a culture that required a physical sacrifice for the atonement of sins, one of the first stories of ultimate sacrifice and worship was when God asked Abraham to sacrifice his son Isaac. For Abraham, this must have been an unbelievable request. But as we know, God was testing Abraham to see if he would give up everything, including the son that God had promised. God set the standard for His expectation of worship.

During the times of the Tabernacle and soon after, the Temple, the process of offering sacrifices and worship was not a simple task. There were many steps involved before coming to the Holy Altar, and it required the guidance and assistance of the holy priests. A thorough study of Exodus through Deuteronomy can outline these very specific and detailed steps.

Davidic praise was a slightly different approach to God.

David's Tabernacle focused on worship through praise, song and music. David and the house of Israel celebrated with "all their might" (2 Samuel 6:14) with songs and instruments.

In the Psalms, we are given many reasons and examples of the worthiness of God. In Psalm 139:14, we "praise you because I am fearfully and wonderfully made." In Psalm 29:2, we "worship the Lord in the splendor of His Holiness." The Psalms reminds us to praise Him because of all His glorious wonder.

Finally in the New Testament, James 5:13 writes that if we are happy we should "sing songs of praise", equating joy with praise. In 1 Corinthians 14:15 Paul says, " I will sing with my spirit...sing with my understanding". And in Ephesians 5:19 (NKJV) and Colossians 3:16 (NKJV), Paul encourages us to sing with "psalms, hymns and spiritual songs".

Reflection

❖ How can we incorporate what we learn from Old Testament and New Testament worship in today's worship services?

6

Worship in Chronicles

"Accompanied by trumpets, cymbals, and other instruments,
the singers raised their voices in praise to the Lord
and sang: 'He is good! His love endures forever'."
2 Chronicles 5:13
Read 1 Chronicles 25:1, 3, 6–8 and 2 Chronicles 5:7–14

In 1 Chronicles 25 we read about some very important imagery and symbolism regarding worship at the Tabernacle. There were priests that were set apart for this specific ministry. Along with music, worship was accompanied with the ministry of prophecy. The priests used instruments like the harps, lyres (an ancient stringed instrument) and cymbals. These priests were trained and skilled. Also, we observe there were no age distinctions; no matter young, old, teacher, or student, all were present for the ministry. Johan Sebastian Bach was an important composer of Christian music. Bach said that 1 Chronicles 25 was the "true foundation for all God pleasing music"[3] and that "music was instituted by the Spirit of God through David".[3] He believed that music was to be used to glorify God. He also acknowledged "where there is devotional music, God is always at hand with His presence."[3]

In 2 Chronicles 5, during the dedication of Solomon's temple, "The trumpeters and singers performed together in unison to praise and give thanks to the Lord. Accompanied by trumpets, cymbals, and other instruments, they raised their voices and praised the Lord with these words: 'He is good! His faithful love endures forever!' At that moment a thick cloud filled the Temple of the Lord. The priests could not continue their service because of the cloud, for the glorious presence of the Lord filled the Temple of God" (v.13–14 NLT). As Solomon had completed the temple construction and was preparing it for dedication, all the appointed priests began to worship with instruments and their voices. Suddenly, God's presence filled the temple, and it was so powerful that the priests could no longer continue!

Worship fosters a holy environment, and the power and the presence of God can be felt. We as worshipers must acknowledge and understand the power of our songs and our music. God doesn't need our worship to show His power, but we can see how in these examples God's glory is manifested through true worship.

Reflection

❖ Is God's power evident in today's worship? In what ways?

7

Revelation/ Heavenly Worship

Day and night they never stop saying:
"Holy, Holy, Holy is the Lord God Almighty,
who was, and is, and is to come.
Revelation 4:8
Read Revelation 4 and 5

When we study the book of Revelation, we see many symbols and representations of worship and music. The sounds that the Apostle John heard in his vision must have been overwhelming. Singing angels used instruments like the harp in worship. Trumpets were sounded in judgment. God's heavenly creations sang songs of worship. John said in Revelation 5:13 that he heard "every creature in heaven and on earth and under the earth and on the sea, and all that is in them, saying: 'To him who sits on the throne and to the Lamb be praise and honor and glory and power for ever and ever!'" Every nation and race was represented in heavenly worship. "A great multitude that no one could count, from every nation, tribe, people and language, standing before the throne and in front of the lamb" (7:9). The sounds in heaven of people worshiping was like "a great multitude, like the roar of rushing waters" (19:6).

The angels, the elders and the heavenly living creatures fell down and worshiped (5:14, 11:16,19:4). What an amazing sight this will be. But we do not have to wait until we reach heaven to worship like this. By worshiping with all our power and might, and together as one unified body, we can emulate heavenly worship together here on Earth.

Reflection

❖ How can we use Heavenly worship as an example for worship on Earth?

8

Importance of Prayer

You will seek me and find me when you
seek me with all your heart.
Jeremiah 29:13
Read 1 Samuel 1 and 2:1–11

As singers, musicians, and technicians, we may focus on our craft so much that we may begin to forget the subject of our worship. Having a consistent prayer life is vital for the growth of each team member. This communion with God, along with pure heartfelt worship, can ensure that we are in line with God's will and call on our life.

In 1 Samuel 1 and 2, we read about the story of Hannah and her answered prayer in her son, Samuel. Hannah and her husband went to the Lord regularly to offer worship and sacrifices. This was a tradition they held on to year after year. Although she could not have children, she still continued to worship. In fact, she was "pouring out my soul to the Lord" (1 Samuel 1:15). Even in her time of "anguish and grief" (v.16), she worshiped. She "worshiped before the Lord…and the Lord remembered her" and she conceived (v. 19–20). In Hannah's prayer, elements of worship are evident. "My heart rejoices in the Lord; my mouth boasts …for I delight in your deliverance" 1 Samuel 2:1. Hannah shows us that through perseverance, patience, and trusting in the Lord, we can continue worshiping God no matter what our circumstance.

Reflection

- ❖ How can worship and prayer go hand in hand?
- ❖ What are some elements of Hannah's prayer that we can incorporate into our prayer life?

9

Sacrifice of Praise

"Through Jesus, therefore, let us continually
offer to God a sacrifice of praise
—the fruit of lips that openly confess his name."
Hebrews 13:15
Read Genesis 4:1–12

Sacrifices in the Old Testament required sacrificing our best to God. In Old Testament times, it required something prized like the 1st born animal of a flock or the 1st yielding of grains and fruit. Today through Jesus, we no longer need to offer blood sacrifices because He did that once and for all on the cross. However, we can still offer our best through worship. Hebrews 13:15 discusses the 'sacrifice of praise', the 'fruit of our lips', and giving thanks to our God in worship. The intent of our heart with these sacrifices is what matters. When Cain offered his sacrifice (Genesis 4), he brought produce from the soil because he was a farmer. It is not clear if Cain brought the best of his labor. Abel, however, brought the best parts of the firstborn lambs as a sacrifice. We read in Hebrews 11:4 that it was by faith that Abel offered a "better" sacrifice than Cain. Abel was obedient in God's requirements for sacrifice, and more importantly,

God looked at the intent of Abel's heart. To sacrifice the firstborn of the flock is to give up something meaningful or the best. God requires we sacrifice our best for Him. Our heart, our words and our praises all need to be at our best to offer to God. If not, we run the risk of offering a half- hearted sacrifice like the one Cain offered, which we know was unacceptable to God, and this eventually led Cain towards the path of sin.

In Romans 12:1 Paul says that you should "offer your bodies as a living sacrifice, holy and pleasing to God". This can be achieved through the physical and spiritual act of worship, humbling ourselves in worship, and by trying to lead a holy life through the guidance of the Holy Spirit. Long ago, only the pure and unblemished were brought for sacrifice. Now that we offer our praise as sacrifice, we must ensure that our hearts are pure and holy.

Reflection

❖ How can we offer our best to God as a sacrifice? On stage/ during worship? In our personal lives?

Qualities & Characteristics
of the Team Member

10

We Are the Body of Christ

So in Christ we, though many, form one body,
and each member belongs to the others.
Romans 12:5
Read 1 Corinthians 12:12–31

In our bodies, every part and organ has a specific function. All our body systems work cohesively together to make sure we are at our optimum health. 1 Corinthians 12 discusses one body with many parts. Paul uses the analogy of our body, its many different parts and functions, and correlates that with each one of us having an important role in the church. Each member of the body of Christ has a particular function, but we must remember that we are also part of the whole church body.

There are various roles in the church. Every one of us has a God-given talent or gift. In 1 Corinthians 12:28–30 Paul says "God has placed in the church first of all apostles, second prophets, third teachers, then miracles, then gifts of healing, of helping, of guidance, and of different kinds of tongues. Are all apostles? Are all prophets? Are all teachers? Do all work miracles? Do all have gifts of healing? Do all speak in tongues? Do all interpret?" We must each understand our unique and vital role within the church, and how every one of us has a part in it. As a choir, we each bring our talents and gifts to the team. Although we must grow and learn to utilize all the talents God has given us, we must also respect and recognize each other's gifts so that we are unified. As we spend more and more time with God, our roles will become more evident to us.

In Romans 12:1 (NKJV), Paul discusses our "reasonable service" as a way of worshiping God. We must utilize the gifts and responsibilities God has entrusted us with to ensure that the church duties are performed. This is our reasonable service of worship.

Reflection

❖ List some "visible" and "not so visible" roles in the church. Can the church function efficiently without them?

11

Qualities of the Worship Leader

Instead, whoever wants to become great among you must be
your servant, and whoever wants to be first must be your
slave— just as the Son of Man did not come to be served,
but to serve, and to give his life as a ransom for many."
Mathew 20:26–28
Read Galatians 5:22–26

To be an effective leader, we must lead by example. Just as Jesus washed the feet of his disciples, we must not only be ready to serve our worship team, but we must serve the congregation as well. The commitment and sacrifice of the leader is immeasurable. The leader must take great care not to overlook the needs of the team while attending to his/her administrative duties. The leader also must ensure that he/she is leading a life that is worthy of a minister in the church. "Self discipline is an absolutely essential element for the effective worship leader".[4]

In the Old Testament, we can study the roles and responsibilities of the Levitical priests. To ensure that all the functions were maintained, each division of priests had very specific roles; whether it was for the transportation of the tabernacle and its contents, or the preparation of the sacrifices or tabernacle furnishings (Numbers 3 and 4). Likewise under the new covenant, we as worship leaders, pastors, elders, and deacons each have specific roles and responsibilities, to ensure that all the functions of the church are handled appropriately, according to God's gift to each.

As a worship leader, we are responsible for engaging the congregation in worship. We cannot however force worship to occur. Leading worship is about preparing the hearts of the people to focus on God. When the focus turns to the leader or the team, then we are misleading the people. When we allow the focus to be directed at God, we have accomplished our goals.

The worship leader's life should be one of holiness and humility. Paul reminds us in 2 Thessalonians 3:9 that as leaders we should "offer ourselves as a model for you to imitate." We should see ourselves as ministers of God with specific duties, just like the priests in the Bible had specified duties. Below is a chart that compares the role of the worship leader to the responsibilities of the Levitical Priests.

Worship Leader Responsibility[5]	Old Testament Priestly Correlate
1) Administration of worship[5]	→ responsible for overseeing sacrificial offerings
2) Instruction of congregation in worship[5]	→ instructed how and which sacrifice to offer
3) Proclamation of the Word in worship[5]	→ reading of the Word/ educating the people
4) Facilitating congregational participation[5]	→ enforcing mosaic law/ corporate and festival worship

Reflection

- ❖ How can the worship leader lead by example?
- ❖ Is this limited solely to the worship leader?
- ❖ How can all members of the worship team lead by example?

12

Qualities of the Worship Team Members (Choir/ Musicians/ AV- Media)

Whatever you do, work at it with all your heart, as working for the Lord...
Colossians 3:23

Romans 12:11 says "never be lacking in zeal, but keep your spiritual fervor, serving the Lord." Fervor also refers to enthusiasm. When we use our talents to glorify God, there is something special and fulfilling that occurs within us. When we lack that enthusiasm, we lose sight of the purpose of our gifts. Colossians 3:23 echoes Ecclesiastes 9:10 which says "whatever your hand finds to do, do it with all your might." There will be times when we feel the pressures of our daily lives and the "grind" can become overwhelming. We might even question the purpose of our gifts and its effectiveness. 1 Corinthians 15:58 says, "Always give yourselves fully to the work of the Lord, because you know that your labor in the Lord is not in vain." 1 Peter 4:10 also says, "Each of you should use whatever gift you have received to serve others, as faithful stewards of God's grace in its various forms." When we use our talents for God's purpose, He will acknowledge and bless our efforts.

As with the worship leader, you are the most successful in leading worship when the focus is not on you but on God. We are not entertainers performing. We must also worship. It is not only the responsibility of the worship leader to lead worship. The congregation will worship through our example. If the church sees you worshiping, they will be encouraged to worship along with you.

Remember, we are not merely musicians or vocalists, but we are a "royal priesthood" (1 Peter 2:9) with a great responsibility. 1 Samuel 10:5 shows us prophets that were also musicians, playing the "lyres, tambourines, flutes and harps...prophesying." In those times, the musicians and worshipers were not laypeople but specially appointed priests! How wonderful is it that God has appointed us so that we can continue to lead His people into worship and into a closer relationship with Him.

Reflection

❖ In what ways can we exemplify "fervor" as part of the worship team? In our personal lives?

13

Living a Holy Life

For God did not call us to be impure, but to live a holy life.
1 Thessalonians 4:7
Read Mathew 5–7

One of the main responsibilities of the worship team is to help lead the congregation into worship. Throughout his letters, Paul discusses the expectations as followers of Christ and classifies us as a royal priesthood (1 Peter 2:9). When we consider ourselves in this way, living a holy life is the only natural path we can take. God's calling in our lives drives us to strive to live a holy and pure life. Paul gives us examples such as honesty, compassion, kindness, humility, gentleness, patience, forgiveness, love, thankfulness (Colossians 3:1–17), respectfulness, a peaceful nature, encouragement, helpfulness, and joy (1 Thessalonians 5:12–28).

Jesus gives us great examples and teachings when we study the Sermon on the Mount (Mathew 5–7). He gives us insight on how to live a holy life. He tells us that the meek, the merciful, the pure in heart, and the peacemakers are blessed. He warns us against anger, lust, retaliation, and revenge. He asks us to love our enemies and give to the needy. Finally, he tells us not to worry about our needs, and to stop judging others. By continuing to read the Word of God, we can see there are many additional ways to lead a holy life. When we use Paul's instructions and the Sermon on the Mount as a guideline, we can be closer to emulating the life Jesus wanted us to lead.

<u>Reflection</u>

❖ What are some challenges preventing us from living a holy life and how can we overcome them?

14

Personal Worship — Personal Devotion

Come near to God and He will come near to you.
James 4:8

In professions that work with machinery or specialized equipment, trained personnel must check their machines routinely in order to ensure they are working at optimal levels. This is known as calibration. Calibrating the instruments may require time, specific testing, and maintenance. If the instruments were not calibrated regularly, the test results would progressively become inaccurate, and the machines would become ineffective.

Daily worship is like this. In order to be in tune with God and His will, we need to have routine worship and time spent in His Word. This is the only way we can function properly. Spending time with God in worship, with prayer and studying the Word, recalibrates us and helps us tune in to God's will in our lives.

Just being on the worship team or part of a church ministry is not enough. This is like telling the congregation that they should only pray and worship on Sunday mornings during the service. Just as the members of the congregation need to have a daily walk with God, the worship team must spend personal time with God. By having personal devotion, you will begin to see God's power and will become evident in your life. Devotion time with the team is important; your personal daily devotion is vital.

Reflection

❖ What can be achieved by daily personal worship/devotion?

❖ Do you feel your personal devotion time is adequate? How can you improve it?

15

The "Heart" of Worship

Love the Lord with all your heart and with
all your soul and with all your strength.
Deuteronomy 6:5

Paul ends both Colossians 3:16 and Ephesians 5:19–20 by saying that we must sing spiritual songs, hymns, and psalms with gratitude and thanks. This is referring to heart of the worshiper. To only sing the songs during our worship is not enough. Our hearts must be grateful and thankful to God. 1 Samuel 16:7 tells us that "the Lord looks at the heart."

Whatever is in our hearts, it will be evident from what comes out of our mouths. Luke 6:45 (NKJV) says, "A good man out of the good treasure of his heart brings forth good... For out of the abundance of the heart his mouth speaks." We may be able to intentionally disguise our true feelings, but this cannot be hidden from God. In Isaiah 29:13 the Lord says "These people come near to me with their mouth and honor me with their lips, but their hearts are far from me. Their worship of me is based on merely human rules they have been taught."

Why does God look at the heart? Our heart is the keeper of our true feelings and intentions, our secret desires, and whether we want to do good or be disobedient. God does not show favoritism, but God sees the intent in our hearts. Perhaps this is the reason why King David was so blessed in all his endeavors. 1 Samuel 13:14 says that David was "a man after God's own heart." He was allowed to put on priestly robes. On one occasion, he was able to eat the bread that only the priests were allowed to eat (1 Samuel 21:1–6, Mark 2:25–26). Why did God allow this? God knew David's heart. He knew that David's one and only intention was to serve and worship the one true living God with all his heart, soul, and strength. So what does God require from our hearts? Jesus said in Mathew 22:37, that the greatest commandment is to "Love the Lord with all your heart and with all your soul and with all your mind."

Psalm 51:16–17 says, "You do not delight in sacrifice, or I would bring it; you do not take pleasure in burnt offerings. My sacrifice, O God, is a broken spirit; a broken and contrite heart you, God, will not despise." Contrite means feelings of regret and sorrow. God looks at the heart of our worship. If our heart is broken and contrite, and we come before His throne in worship, then we truly are offering up our sacrifices with our heart. Psalm 24:3–4 asks, "Who may ascend the mountain of the Lord? Who may stand in His holy place? The one who has clean hands and a pure heart." We can ascend to His holy place and become closer to Him, only if our heart is pure and in the right place, and is seeking God. How can we keep a pure heart? By coming to his throne with a contrite spirit, and by keeping his Word in our hearts. Hebrews 4:12 says "For the word of God is alive and active. Sharper than any double-edged sword, it penetrates even to dividing soul and spirit, joints and marrow; it judges the thoughts and attitudes of the heart." The Word of God can judge our hearts and purify us, so that we can become repentant and come closer to God.

Reflection

❖ What is the state of the heart of the worshiper today?
❖ Where is your heart as you lead/sing/play during worship?

16

Discipline — Part I
Solitude & The Word

*Now in the morning, having risen a
long while before daylight,
He went out and departed to a solitary
place; and there He prayed.
Mark 1:35 (NKJV)*

Although we only need to look at Jesus' sacrifice as our saving grace and understand that our actions will not qualify us for salvation, we must learn to practice certain disciplines to strengthen our Christian walk. There are various disciplines, and certain disciplines may speak differently to each of us. Psychiatrist Scott Peck captures the struggle with Christians today. He says that we have the vision and desire but "lack the will".[6] We want to "skip over the discipline, to find an easy shortcut to sainthood."[6] Just as an athlete needs to train extensively and with discipline for an athletic event, we as Christians must train and prepare ourselves for the tests of daily living. We can only achieve this through practicing disciplines that will help us grow in our spirituality and ultimately strengthen our faith. Below are a few important disciplines:

1) <u>Silence & Solitude</u>

There is something about being in silence that allows us time to reflect. Sometimes we do our best thinking when we are alone. When in silence, we are away from outside distractions, which allows us to think freely. God asks us to be still and silent so that we can hear Him (Psalm 46:10). Jesus spent a lot of time in solitude. In Luke 5:16 (NKJV) we see Jesus "...withdrew into the wilderness and prayed." In Mark 6:32 Jesus and the disciples "went away by themselves in a boat to a solitary place." And in Mathew 14:13, Jesus "withdrew by boat privately to a solitary place." Solitude is a great source of strength, especially for the maturing Christian. "Silence will allow us life-transforming concentration upon God. It allows us to hear the gentle God".[7]

2) <u>Spending Time in the Word</u>

Most of us are looking for a personal relationship with God, where we seek His guidance for our lives. But God does not always speak to us in the audible sense. God does, however, speak to us through His Word. To study the Word is to nourish ourselves spiritually, just as eating food nourishes us physically.[8] To spend time in his Word is to know the will of God. The Word of God is like an instruction manual for our daily living. Not reflecting on God's Word is like cooking a new meal without a recipe. You kind of muddle through and hope you get it right. But we don't have to live like that. God asks us to keep His Word in our hearts. Psalm 119:11 says, "I have hidden your word in my heart that I might not sin against you." By studying and keeping His word in our heart, we will be reminded of it during difficult times.

Reflection

❖ What are some distractions that prevent us from being in silence and solitude with God?

❖ What are the benefits of spending time in worship and in the Word in solitude?

17

Discipline — Part II
Prayer & Fasting

Do not conform to the pattern of this world,
but be transformed by the renewing of the mind.
Romans 12:2

3) <u>Prayer</u>

We've discussed the importance of prayer in Week 8. But prayer as a discipline is something we must put into practice so that it can become a routine part of our lives. Jesus instructs us in Mathew 6:6 (NKJV) "But you, when you pray, go into your room, and when you have shut your door, pray to your Father who is in the secret place; and your Father who sees in secret will reward you openly." Jesus himself prayed regularly. Luke 6:12 (NKJV) tells us "He went out to the mountain to pray, and continued all night in prayer to God." The discipline of prayer allows us to be continuously connected to God.

4) <u>Fasting</u>

We find sustenance in God through fasting. Jesus, Paul, and the disciples fasted, prayed and practiced being in solitude. Jesus was strengthened, not weakened, because of his solitude and fasting. Fasting is meant for us to clear our minds and to focus on God. Fasting traditionally means avoiding meals for a time period. But it doesn't have to be limited to just food or meals. We can also give up time spent on television, technology, and other activities. The point is, that during this time of fasting you should be focusing and spending time with God. If we fast but continue with our daily activities as usual, then we lose the chance to make a special connection with God and miss the benefit of fasting.

The disciplines are meant for us to build a stronger relationship with God. When practicing a specific discipline we must take care not to forget it's intent, so that "the activities constituting the disciplines have no value in themselves".[9] If we practice these disciplines because of routine and without purpose, then we miss the point. Christian philosopher Dr. Dallas Willard compares this to a "person obsessed with diet or bodybuilding, [it is] no longer about health or strength." It is "muscle for muscle's sake".[10]

<u>Reflection</u>

❖ If we follow these and other disciplines, how can we ensure that they won't lose their value?

18

Musicianship – Work Hard, Practice Hard

Do you see someone skilled in their work?
They will serve before kings;
they will not serve before officials of low rank.
Proverbs 22:29
Read Romans 12:1–8

Romans 12:6–8 discusses many of our various gifts; "We have different gifts, according to the grace given to each of us. If your gift is prophesying, then prophesy in accordance with your faith; if it is serving, then serve; if it is teaching, then teach; if it is to encourage, then give encouragement; if it is giving, then give generously; if it is to lead, do it diligently; if it is to show mercy, do it cheerfully." God gives us various gifts and talents. Even if we share similar talents, he made us unique, with different skills and experiences. He did not give us special talents so that it could be wasted away. He wants us to develop our skills, and ultimately use them for His glory.

There is a standard of excellence when it comes to the things of God. He requires it, and we should demand it from ourselves. Colossians 3:23 says, "whatever you do, work at it with all your heart, as working for the Lord." But we cannot expect excellence without preparation. We must take care not to become like the man in Proverbs 20:4 (NLT) which warns "those too lazy to plow in the right season will have no food at the harvest."

In the creation of the tabernacle, we see extraordinary detail, from fine linens and special colors used for the coverings and curtains, to the woodwork and metalwork. God anointed specialized craftsmen and designers to perform the task of building the tabernacle (Exodus 25–27 and 30). God told Moses to make the tabernacle exactly to the specifications given. The writer of Hebrews says that the temple and tabernacle were copies of what was in Heaven. God replicated the beauty of these things because this is what is in heaven! God blessed us with unique specialized talents that he wants to see used for His glory. He gave it to us, because he sees the beauty of it in us. Knowing this, how can we not use our talents to glorify Him everyday? 1 Chronicles 25:7 shows us priests that were "**trained** and skilled in music for the Lord." Training means practicing our craft and developing our God given gifts. We all have certain raw talents, some more developed than others. But we can always fine tune and be better at our crafts. We do this so that we may glorify the Kingdom of God.

Reflection

❖ If God has already given us the talent, then why do we need to practice or improve in our crafts?

19

Confidence

Have I not commanded you? Be strong and of good courage.
Do not be afraid, nor be dismayed, for the Lord
your God is with you wherever you go.
Joshua 1:9 (NKJV)
Read Exodus 3 and 4:1–17

When God called Moses to lead His people out of Egypt, we see that Moses lacked confidence. In Exodus 4, Moses wanted signs and confirmations from God. And even after God appeased him with these, Moses still lacked the courage. Eventually, we know that Moses, with his faith in God, led the Israelites out of Egypt. As the successor to Moses, God appointed Joshua to lead his people over the Jordan River into the His Promised Land. We read many times that God encouraged Joshua to trust in him. "Be strong and courageous," God said (Joshua 1:6,7,9). Sometimes, when we are given certain responsibilities, we doubt our capabilities. We begin to doubt ourselves, and question if we are qualified or skilled. God has given each of us talents and gifts. His expectation is for us to use them. Of course, there is always room for us to fine tune our skills and become better. But to not use our gifts because of our lack of confidence is a waste of our talents and doubting in God's plan over our lives.

In Mathew 25:14–30 Jesus tells us of the story of the master and servants he entrusted with 'talents' (a form of currency). The servant that was given one talent hid it away instead of investing it (in fear of losing it), and was cursed by the master. We should not be afraid to use the 'talents' that God has given to us. Learn to use them in confidence to glorify his kingdom. "I can do all things through Christ who strengthens me" Philippians 4:13 (NKJV).

Reflection

❖ What prevents us from utilizing our talents for God?
❖ How can we overcome this?

20

Humility

Do nothing out of selfish ambition or vain conceit.
Rather, in humility value others above yourselves,
not looking to your own interests but each
of you to the interests of the others.
Philippians 2:3–4
Read 2 Chronicles 26 and Daniel 4:28–37

As musically inclined individuals, we tend to "march to our own beat". This trait however, can have positive and negative implications. We must learn to have the ability to listen and to be taught by others. This can only come with respect for our leaders, pastors, and members of the team, as well as for the congregation. Of course this comes with the understanding that there needs to be mutual respect for all parties and viewpoints involved.

Look at the life of King Uzziah. 2 Chronicles 26:4 says Uzziah "did what was right in the eyes of the Lord." Because he was obedient to God, God gave him success in everything he did (v.5). Unfortunately, he became prideful because of his power. He became so proud that he did not respect the role of the appointed priests and tried to burn incense at the Altar of the temple, a strictly priestly function. As a result of his pride and disobedience, God punished him with leprosy. "A boy turned king and seeker of God, turned proud man, turned profane burner of incense, turned leper."[11] He went from being a king to being an outcast (v.21).

King Nebuchadnezzar also became proud of his kingdom and his accomplishments, even though Daniel had warned him. Because of his arrogance, God humbled him (Daniel 4:31). Only after this did Nebuchadnezzar acknowledge the one true God and humbled himself before the Lord.

Ephesians 4:2–3 reminds us to "Be completely humble and gentle; be patient, bearing with one another in love. Make every effort to keep the unity of the Spirit through the bond of peace." God tells Isaiah in 66:2 "These are the ones I look on with favor: those who are humble and contrite in spirit, and who tremble at my word." "Humility is the teacher of all the virtues; it is the most firm foundation of the heavenly edifice; it is the Savior's own magnificent gift."[12]

Reflection

❖ What are some things we can do to keep ourselves "in check" from becoming arrogant and staying humble?

❖ Personally and as a team?

21

Focus on God, Not Ourselves

...in the last days there will come times of difficulty. For people will be lovers of self...proud, arrogant... swollen with conceit, lovers of pleasure rather than lovers of God, having the appearance of godliness, but denying its power.
2 Timothy 3:1–7 (ESV)

A growing concern of the church today is what we can call "spiritual narcissism". The focus of spirituality becomes primarily on the individual and not on God. We may ask questions like:

- "Did I like the preacher's message?"
- "How did it affect me?"
- "How was the worship team?"
- "Did I like their song selections?"
- "What programs and activities does this church have for me?"

"Spirituality becomes narcissistic when one becomes fascinated with his or her own journey and gives priority to self-reflection."[13] We can see this with the worship team as well, asking questions like:

- "How was worship today?"
- "How was my vocal/ guitar/ drum solo?"

Instead we should be asking questions like:

- "Was my worship pleasing to God?"
- "Did I worship with all my might?"
- "Did our worship lead people to experience God and have a closer connection with Him?"

We sometimes look for audience approval and appreciation, instead of being concerned if God's presence is being felt and true worship is occurring. "Worship is not measured by the depth of my feelings, but the deep wonder of the God whose story is so marvelous that it does in fact create feelings of love and gratitude".[14]

An example of this can be seen in King Saul. He was the 1st chosen King of Israel, selected by God (1 Samuel 9). But his arrogance got the best of him, and he sought to expand his kingdom and to please his followers. He even "set up a monument in his own honor" (1 Samuel 15:12). We see in his life that he chose to do sacrifices rather than be obedient to God (1 Samuel 15:20–23). He did not seek God in his decisions. He may have thought he was doing the right thing. Although his intentions may have been honorable, his heart was not right – and God knows our heart and intentions.

What are your intentions for being on the worship team? We may have started out with good intentions, but are we on the team currently for the right reasons? Our focus must always stay on God, not on ourselves or even on the team. God tells us that "arrogance [is] like the evil of idolatry" (1

Dr. A. Ben Cheriyan

Samuel 15:23). Arrogance and narcissism is idolatry, because we are worshiping ourselves!

<u>Reflection</u>

❖ It is very easy to focus on ourselves, whether intentionally or unintentionally. What can we do to make sure we keep our focus on God?

Expressions of Worship

22

Role of Music

Sing and make music...
Psalm 27:6, 57:7, 108:1; Ephesians 5:19

"Music can, and often does, convey a greater intensity of feeling than would be expressed in its absence".[15] Music plays a significant role in many functions and events. When music is being played, it adds another element to the setting, even if it is on a subconscious level. This is apparent in various situations in society. It can mark the beginning or end to an event. It is played at sporting events, ceremonial events, and formal and informal gatherings. Music can shift the mood of an event. Even during the service, we see some churches may use an instrumentalist to play in the background while the minister is speaking.

In 2 Kings 3, we read the story of Elisha meeting with the kings of Israel, Judah, and Edom. They had run out of water for their soldiers and animals, and although they worshiped idols, they were desperate and sought out Elisha and God. (Do we also go our own ways, and then seek the Lord in our time of trouble?) Elisha then calls on a harpist, and while the harpist played, the "hand of the Lord came on

Elisha" and he was able to prophesize about water for them and their future victory.

After God had disinherited King Saul because of his disobedience, an evil spirit tormented him. We see the only way that he found any peace was when David played the harp for him (1 Samuel 16:23).

Even Jesus mentions music in a celebratory reference through the parable of the prodigal son in Luke 15:25, "Meanwhile, the older son was in the field. When he came near the house, he heard music and dancing." Throughout the Bible, it is evident that music has a particular significance and importance.

Reflection

❖ When can music enhance the service and when can it be a distraction?

23

Why Do We Sing?

Singing psalms, hymns and spiritual songs…
Colossians 3:16 (ESV)
Read 2 Chronicles 20:1–29

Why do we sing when we worship? Can't we just play music and spend quiet time with God? Although there is value in quiet reflection, there is power in songs that are sung to the Lord. We sing to praise. We sing to worship and to commune with God. We sing as one voice and as one body with the congregation. We should not sing because the songs sound good and are pleasing to us, or because we have specific preferences for songs.

David wrote the Psalms, in times of joy and in times of despair. The Psalms give abundant examples of singing praises to God. Solomon may have been known for his proverbs, but he wrote many songs as well. 1 Corinth 14:15 (ESV) says, "I will sing praise with my spirit, but I will sing with my mind also." Ephesians 5:19 tells us to "sing and make music from your heart to the Lord." James 5:13 asks, "Is anyone happy? Let them sing songs of praise." Jesus sang hymns with his disciples at the last supper (Matthew 26:30). We sing to the Lord, because he is worthy of all our praise.

In 2 Chronicles 20, we see the story of King Jehoshaphat. God was with Jehoshaphat because "he walked in the earlier ways of his father David" (2 Chron. 17:3 ESV). Through a prophet God told Jehoshaphat not to worry about the oncoming attack by the Moabites and Ammonites. In fact, God instructed Jehoshaphat to just sit back and watch! "You will not have to fight this battle. Take up your positions; stand firm and see the deliverance the Lord will give you" (20:17). So Jehoshaphat and his men sang to the Lord and praised him singing "Give thanks to the Lord, for his love endures forever" (v.21). And as they sang, God turned the attackers on themselves and "they to helped destroy one another" (v.23). See the amazing power of God!

Reflection

❖ What does singing do for the worshiper? For the church? For God?

24

Worship Postures, Gestures, & Actions

The Lord is my strength and my song;
and he has become my salvation.
Shouts of joy and victory resound and
the tents of the righteous.
Psalm 118:14–15
Read Exodus 17:8–15

Besides through song and music, we see other expressions of worship throughout the Bible. Today, we may be hesitant or too poised to express worship in these ways. But we see these expressions in Old Testament worship (especially in David's time) as well as in the New Testament church.

Many examples of worship in the Bible, especially in the Psalms, are of joyous celebrations and awe-filled adoration and worship; where people clap, lift up hands, shout to the lord, dance and lift up banners. The book of Psalms describes various worship styles. We also observe many different physical acts of worship. We can see that worshiping God was not only meant for standing still, or worshiping in a somber or remorseful state—although there are times when that kind of worship is appropriate.

Some expressions include:

- Shouting — Psalms 42:4 and 118:15
- Lifting up banners — Psalm 20:5
- Bowing — Psalm 95:6
- Clapping — Psalms 98:8 and 47:1
- Lifting up hands — Psalms 141:2, 28:2, 134:2, 63:4, and 119:48
- Spreading out hands — Psalms 88:9 and 143:6
- Kneeling — Ephesians 3:14
- Jumping — Acts 3:8
- Dancing — Psalms 149:3 and 150:4
- Singing aloud — Psalm 95:1–2
- Liturgical responses like "Amen, Hallelujah, and Praise the Lord" were all common responses made from the people during worship, whether it was in affirmation to the worship or speaker's words, or spontaneous worship to God.[16]

As worship leaders, it is our responsibility that all aspects of worship are cultivated. Praising God through uplifting songs, shouts of joy, songs of reverence, worship and adoration, crying out and bowing down before our Maker, should all be included in our worship as our heart and the Spirit leads us.

Reflection

- ❖ Are there defined times when a worshiper should be expressive in their worship?
- ❖ What kinds of expressions are encouraged during your worship?

25

Voices/ Choirs

Then I looked, and I heard the voice of many angels around
the throne, the living creatures and the elders; and the
number of them was ten thousand times ten thousand, and
thousands of thousands, saying with a loud voice, "Worthy
is the Lamb that was slain to receive power and riches and
wisdom and strength and honor and glory and blessing!"
Revelation 5:11–12 (NKJV)
Read 1 Chronicles 15:16–28

The greatest example of a singing choir in the Bible is the
one we see in the book of Revelation. In chapter 5 verse 11,
there are thousands and even tens of thousands of angels
singing and worshiping God on the throne.

In Old Testament times, there were specially trained
and skilled priests that sang and formed a choir for worship
to God. In 1 Chronicles 15:16 (NLT), we see David bringing
the Ark back to Israel, and he "ordered the Levite leaders to
appoint a choir of Levites who were singers and musicians
to sing joyful songs." These were not only priests that had
a desire to sing, but they had the talent and gift to sing.
Verse 22 says "Kenaniah, the head Levite was in charge of
the singing…because he was skillful at it." Verse 27 tells us

the procession consisted of singers shouting, singing and playing instruments.

In the story of Nehemiah, we see that he helped the returning Israelite exiles rebuild the walls of Jerusalem. The walls had been broken down and left the city unprotected. After completing the wall, there was a dedication to God. During that dedication, there was joyful celebration with songs, music, instruments, and choirs. "I had the leaders of Judah go up on top of the wall. I also appointed two large choirs to give thanks," he said in Nehemiah 12:31. "The two choirs that gave thanks took their places in the house of God" (v.40). "The sound of rejoicing in Jerusalem could be heard far away" (v.43).

Reflection

❖ What are the effects/ benefits of having many voices singing along as you lead worship?

26

Musical Instruments

*Praise him with the sounding of the trumpet, praise him with
the harp and lyre, praise him with timbrel and dancing,
praise him with the strings and pipe, praise him with the
clash of cymbals, praise him with resounding cymbals.*
Psalm 150:3–5
Read Joshua 6:1–21

Although there may be debates in our churches on the
validity of using instruments during our worship, the use
of musical instruments and its importance and meaning
in the Bible cannot be ignored. There have been many
instances in the Bible that refer to musical instruments and
its association with worship, praise, and even the power of
God. What musicians and leaders must realize is that the
heart of the worshiper is what is pleasing to God. So whether
your church has one guitar and a tambourine, or a fifty-
member choir and music team, God's spirit can be evident
in a place where true worship happens. Music is meant to be
an accessory for worship, not the driving force.

In Revelation 14:2 the apostle John was seeing a vision
of heaven, "And I heard a sound from heaven like the roar of
rushing waters and like a loud peal of thunder. The sound

I heard was like that of harpists playing their harps." In Revelation 5:8 "the four living creatures and the twenty-four elders fell down before the Lamb. Each one had a harp." Where did these harps come from? Were these instruments that the heavenly beings attained from earth? In Revelation 15:2–3 John says "They held harps **given** them **by God** and sang the song of God's servant Moses and of the Lamb." The Amplified Bible translates this as "with harps **of God** in their hands". We can clearly see that these instruments were created and given by God. In 1 Chronicles 16:42 (NKJV) it says "to sound aloud with trumpets and cymbals and the musical instruments **of** God." In Revelation 8, the seven angels sound their trumpets for punishments and disasters to follow. With these examples, one can easily conclude that instruments have a significant role in heaven.

In 1 Samuel 18:6 "When the men were returning home after David had killed the Philistine, the women came out from all the towns of Israel to meet King Saul with singing and dancing, with joyful songs and with timbrels and lyres." Here music and instruments are associated with joyous celebrations and dancing.

Using instruments were instructed and commanded by God. 2 Chronicles 29:25 says that King Hezekiah "stationed the Levites in the temple of the LORD with cymbals, harps and lyres in the way prescribed by David and Gad the king's seer and Nathan the prophet; **this was commanded by the LORD** through his prophets." Even the walls of Jericho fell at the sounding of the trumpets of the soldiers (Joshua 6:20). David also appointed Levites and said "…four thousand are to praise the lord with the musical instruments" (1 Chronicles 23:5). What a sound that must have been!

<u>Reflection</u>

❖ When can using instruments be a hindrance to worship?
❖ How can we ensure that instruments enhances our worship?

Biblical Influencers of Worship

27

Abraham

One of the first individuals to set the standard for worship was Abraham. In week 5, we read about Abraham and his contribution to worship. Abraham was a righteous man and worshiped God regularly. Because of his righteousness, God chose Abraham to be the father of His people. However, God tested Abraham to see if he was fully committed to Him. If we think about the sacrifice that God had requested, it may seem unimaginable. God wanted to see if Abraham was willing to give up the son that he had waited so long for, the son that God had promised! God tested Abraham to see if He was ready to serve Him with all his might, which meant giving up anything that was important to Abraham. Of course God had no intention of having Isaac sacrificed. He even provided a ram in Isaac's place. Abraham set the bar for worship. His primary goal was to worship and serve God, and he was ready to give up all that meant everything to him. When we serve God, are we willing to give it all up?

Or are we preoccupied with the things we deem important to us—placing God second in our lives.

Thankfully today, God is not requiring us to make these extreme sacrifices. But God does require us to put Him first before anything else. When we worship, we come to his feet and offer ourselves completely to God. Abraham was asked to sacrifice it all, and God is asking us to do the same today, by being willing to give up all we are and all we have to Him.

<u>Reflection</u>

❖ God tested Abraham to see if he was willing to give it all up for him. What can we "sacrifice" to show God that we are "all in"?

28

David

I will exalt you, my God the King; I will
praise your name forever and ever.
Every day I will praise you and extol
your name forever and ever.
Psalm 145:1–2
Read 1 Chronicles 13, 15 and 16

God said that David was a "man after his own heart" (1 Samuel 13:14). Because of David's zeal and love for God, God established a covenant in which He promised, "Your throne shall be established forever" (2 Samuel 7:16). This would be fulfilled through God's son and David's descendent, Jesus.

As a musician, we see David placed a large emphasis on the importance and relevance of music, songs, and instruments in Godly worship. Throughout all the books in the Bible, there is never more of an abundance of references to music and song as there is in the time of David. David was a skilled musician even at a young age. When the Spirit of God had departed from King Saul, an evil spirit entered him and tormented him. His servants suggested finding a skilled musician, and David was chosen from all musicians in the kingdom! "Whenever the spirit from God came on Saul, David would take up his lyre and play. Then relief would come to Saul; he would feel better, and the evil spirit would leave him" 1 Samuel 16:23.

Before David's rule, the Ark of the Covenant was captured by the Philistines (1 Samuel 4). The Ark was then taken to a place called Kiriath Jearim, where it stayed until David became King (1 Chronicles 13:5). David wanted to bring the Ark back to the people of Israel. Unfortunately during the transport (because it was not handled according to God's guidelines (1 Chron. 15:13)), God punished Uzzah, who touched the ark to prevent it from falling. Although Uzzah's intentions were good, his disobedience cost him his life (1 Chron. 13:9–10). When David realized that the proper steps had not been taken to move the Holy Ark, he asked the priests and the Levites to transport it properly. David appointed singers and musicians (Levites) to assist in bringing the Ark back. In 1 Chronicles 13:8 as well as in 15:28, the ark was transported back to Jerusalem with shouts of joy, songs, and music. Through this we can appreciate that the presence of the Lord is not something to be taken lightly. David was also a king without pride. He had put down his royal robes and danced with all his might before the ark, much to the disapproval of his Queen Michal (2 Samuel 6:14-23).

David understood the importance of praising and worshiping God. All he wanted to do was seek God and praise God for all His glory. He worshiped no matter what the situation. We read throughout the Old Testament that he had many troubling times. But David understood the greatest commandment, "worship the Lord your God with all your heart" (Mathew 22:37-38).

Reflection

❖ Why was David's form of worship different from what had already been established?
❖ How can we apply the nature and intent of Davidic worship today?

29

Jesus

He is the image of the invisible God, the firstborn
over all creation. For by him all things are created:
things in heaven and on earth, visible and invisible...;
all things were created by Him and for Him.
And he is before all things, and in him all things
consist. And he is the head of the body, the church...
Colossians 1:15–18 (NKJV)
Read Mathew 26:6–13

Jesus is the reason we can worship the way we do today. He is the subject of our worship. He came down from His Heavenly throne and changed worship entirely. If it were not for Him, we would either be going to the temple to offer worship and sacrifices for the atonement of our sins, or we would possibly not know God at all. But because of His ultimate sacrifice, which He paid in blood, we can now worship God freely. No additional sacrifice can bring us closer to Him. Jesus became the final sacrifice. Upon His death, He tore the veil in the temple that separated man from God, so that we could have a closer relationship with God (Mathew 27:50–51). This was an amazing sign to show that God wanted a more intimate relationship with us again.

In Mathew 26:6–13, we see the story of a woman who anointed Jesus feet with expensive perfume. Jesus said that she had done a "beautiful thing". This was a very expensive gesture, one year's worth of wages. Imagine donating one year's worth of your salary to your church! But this was her ultimate sacrifice. It didn't matter to her how much the perfume was worth. This was her expression of worship and adoration to Jesus. We can imagine that this perfume filled the house with fragrance. When we worship today, it should fill the area we are worshiping in with a holy atmosphere. This can only happen when we give our all in worship, and we are in total adoration of God.

We must study and remember the Old Testament format of worship, and be thankful that we now have freedom to worship because of what Jesus did for us on the cross. Jesus also sang songs, prayed, fasted, and worshiped during His time here on Earth. He showed us that worshiping God is an important aspect of growing in our faith.

<u>Reflection</u>

❖ As a team, how can we ensure that our worship leads to a focus on Jesus?
❖ What are some examples Jesus gave on how we can worship?

30

Peter

Instead, you must worship Christ as Lord of your life.
And if someone asks about your hope as a
believer, always be ready to explain it.
1 Peter 3:15 (NLT)
Read Mathew 14:22–32 and John 21

Peter was a zealous and passionate individual. This is apparent when we read about his demeanor and actions as a disciple. Peter had the characteristics of boldness and bravery. One example of this is when he drew his sword and cut the ear of a soldier as they came to arrest Jesus (John 18:10). But his boldness disappeared when he was questioned about his faith; making him deny the very Savior he was passionate about (Luke 22:54–62).

Another example of his passion for Christ was when he jumped into the water after Jesus (Mathew 14:22-32). Jesus was walking on water, a feat no man had ever done on Earth. Yet Peter had faith that he too could walk on water as long as Jesus called him. And for a short time, he did! Unfortunately, because the wind and waves were strong, he was afraid and began to sink. But when he saw Jesus, he reached out and grabbed His hand, and he was saved. He learned that Jesus was there for him, even in his time of doubt. Later we see that Peter doesn't hesitate and jumps boldly into the water after Jesus (John 21:7). Peter's faith strengthened as he learned to depend on Jesus more.

We can be bold and passionate about serving God, but we must learn to trust in Jesus at all times. Many times Jesus tells us "fear not". Jesus said to Peter "Ye of little faith, why did you doubt?" Boldness is incomplete without faith. If we completely trust in Him, and we are bold and passionate, our faith will be complete.

When times are tough, can we still worship God? When there are added pressures and stresses in our lives, will we run away like Peter, and deny Jesus our time and our worship? Or are we at a point in our lives where we can boldly stand up and say "I will trust in the Lord and fear no evil." With the help of the Holy Spirit, Peter unified his faith and boldness. On the day of Pentecost, Peter, filled with the power of the Holy Spirit, boldly and bravely stood up and proclaimed the Good News.

In 1 Peter 3, Peter gives us advice to be able to explain our faith to others if questioned. He did not have this assurance early on his faith, but he was strengthened as he grew deeper in his relationship with God.

Reflection

❖ What are some things that happen in our lives that may make us falter with our walk with God?
❖ How can we strengthen our faith so that we can endure these tough trials?

31

Paul

*Speaking to one another with psalms, hymns and songs from
the Spirit. Sing and make music from your heart to the Lord,
always giving thanks to God the Father for everything,
in the name of our Lord Jesus Christ.*
Ephesians 5:19–20
Read Acts 16:16–40

Even though we don't traditionally think of Paul as a
worship leader, he gives us a lot of insight on the power and
role of worship in the church and in our lives. We see in 1
Corinthians 14:26–39 he advises the Corinthian church on
the order of worship. He also gives specific instructions on
worship, for example "men everywhere to pray, lifting up
holy hands" (1 Timothy 2:8). In Romans 12, Paul tells us
that our bodies (or personal lives) and acts of worship are
like living sacrifices. And in Colossians 3:16 he reminds us
to sing "with gratitude in your hearts".

One of the more familiar examples of worship in Paul's
life is the story of when Paul and Silas were thrown in prison
(Acts 16). Through their prayer and singing of hymns,
the power of God came upon that prison. There was a
violent earthquake and the foundations were shaken. Their

chains were loosed and broken while they were singing and praising God!

Paul's letters in the New Testament are studied thoroughly by Christians. His letters give us instructions on how to lead a holy life, and advice for daily Christian living. He advises how to handle issues, temptations and worldly influences. Paul was a disciplined and well-educated Jewish scholar. His advice gives us practical applications for our Christian walk, and it can help us to become more effective worshipers.

<u>Reflection</u>

❖ Discuss Paul's "spiritual act of worship" in Romans 12.
❖ Discuss Paul's impact on Christianity, despite his infamous past (Acts 8:1–3; 9:1–17).

Leading in the Spirit

32

River of God – Part I

Whoever believes in me, as Scripture has said, rivers
of living water will flow from within them.
John 7:38
Read Ezekiel 47

In Ezekiel 47, the prophet Ezekiel describes his vision of a river flowing from the temple of God. Even though he does not mention the width of the river, we can estimate its width based on the description of the various depths. In his book Worship That Pleases God[17], Dr. Stephen Phifer explains that this river can be used as a model for worship—where the different depths of the river can correlate to different depths of worship.

In the River of Life model, there are different levels of worship. According to Ezekiel's vision, there was quite a distance between each level of depth in the river. It would take some time to tread these waters to get to the next level. We can compare this to our worship. Worship is a journey and not something that can be rushed into, achieved at a moment's notice, or planned within a specified time in the service. Careful time and reflection must be spent before getting to the "next" level of worship.[17]

1st Level[17]

We see the angel of God leading Ezekiel to the first depth, which is ankle deep. This can correlate in today's worship as thanksgiving to God. In the Old Testament temple, we enter His gates with thanksgiving, which is the first step to get closer to the Holy of Holies. When we enter the church service, we can start by giving praise and thanks to God. Psalm 50:14 tells us to "sacrifice thank offerings to God."

2nd Level[17]

As Ezekiel is led to the next level, the angel measures out 1000 cubits. This is equivalent to 1500 feet or 5 football fields! We can assume that it takes some time to get to the next level. It cannot be rushed, just like our worship cannot be rushed. This level is knee deep. It signifies exaltation to God. To exalt means to glorify. After we give Him thanksgiving, we must glorify Him through our worship. We exalt by lifting up His name, because He is worthy.

Reflection

- ❖ How can we set up our worship services to achieve the different levels of worship?
- ❖ Do you have freedom to allow the congregation to worship, even if it is not within an allotted time in the service?

33

River of God – Part II

There is a river whose streams make glad the city of
God, the holy place where the Most High dwells.
Psalm 46:4
Read Ezekiel 47

Last week we learned about the River of Life discussed in Ezekiel 47. We see that there are four different depths in the river. Each depth is 1000 cubits wide, or 1500 feet, the length of 5 football fields each! We can correlate this with different levels of worship. Ankle deep in the River signifies we are worshiping with thanksgiving. Knee deep in the River, we glorify and exalt God.

3rd Level[17]

At the next level, we see is Ezekiel is led through the River up to his waist. This can symbolize the adoration of God. When you are waist deep in water, you are quite immersed. At this point in worship, after thanksgiving and exaltation, we are in awe and adoration of God.

4th Level[17]

The last level/ depth is when the River runs overhead. This means that the water is deep enough to swim. Now we are completely immersed in worship, and we commune with God. Dr. Phifer indicates once you have entered this depth and distance in the River, you cannot go back to the same place from where you entered.[17] True worship can change our perspective, our position, and our attitude about things going on in our lives. True worship will bring you to a different place. As we commune with God, we become closer to Him.

Using the River as a model for worship, we can see how we cannot be the same after experiencing His overflowing abundance in worship. This is how deep worship and communion with Him can be spirit-lifting and life-altering.[17]

Reflection

- ❖ Is there enough time dedicated during our services to experience all these levels of worship? If not, why?
- ❖ How can the songs we sing help us through these different levels of worship?

34

Spirit & Truth

Yet a time is coming and has now come when the true
worshipers will worship the Father in the Spirit and in truth,
for they are the kind of worshipers the Father seeks. God is
Spirit, and his worshipers must worship in spirit and in truth.
John 4:23–24
Read John 4:19–26

Romans 12:2 (NKJV) says "do not to be conformed to this world." Worshiping in the spirit is to concentrate on Him and to let go of all worldly distractions. We allow God's Spirit, the Holy Spirit, to commune with our spirit. When we worship Him with all our power and might, and we can let go of all worldly things and worship freely, it becomes spirit-filled worship or heavenly worship. We must heed Jesus' warnings and be careful not to follow the actions of the Pharisees in Mathew 15:8. He said "these people honor me with their lips but their hearts are far from me." When we worship with a pure heart and are fully focused on God, it allows us to be in tune with the Holy Spirit. As worshipers, this increases our sensitivity to the Spirit and His direction. As leaders, it is vital we lead the congregation with the guidance of the Holy Spirit.

Worshiping in Truth requires us to know God through His Word. By spending time in the Word, we begin to know our God and learn His ways, His will and His expectations for our lives. In John 4:22, Jesus tells the Samaritan women that they do not know who they worship. In truth and His Word, we discover who God is. 1 Corinthians 14:15 says that we should "sing with my spirit...but I will also sing with my understanding." By understanding the will of God through His Word, and allowing the Holy Spirit to lead the service, we can lead the congregation in both Spirit and Truth worship.

Reflection

- ❖ What kind of worshiper are you? Spirit or Truth?
- ❖ How can you achieve a balance of both?
- ❖ How can you lead your church into worship in both Spirit and Truth?

35

Leading the Congregation Into Worship

Glorify the Lord with me; Let us exalt his name together.
Psalm 34:3
Read 1 Chronicles 15 and 16:36

Leading the congregation is not just the responsibility of the worship leader or the pastor. The whole team—including the choir, musicians, sound team, lights and video teams—all share in this great responsibility. Together, we lead the church into worship. As we fix our eyes on heaven and worship, so will the congregation. We must focus on the worship and on God, and not on the nuances that go with singing, playing music, and technological issues. Even when we play our best, and despite all our preparation, there may still be unpredictable and unavoidable issues. Our preparation is not what allows congregants to feel His presence, but it is the heart and mind of the worshiper (including the teams') that allows us to experience Him.

When on stage or leading worship, we may concentrate on musicianship so much that we tend to forget the focus and subject of our worship. Yes, we must make sure that we play and perform all our functions to the best of our abilities. But we are not entertainers. We are worshipers of a

Living God. Leading the congregation can be like leading a loved one through a crowd. Together, we get past the crowd, despite any distractions, to reach the destination. This is the relationship of the worship team and the congregation. We worship with each other to reach our final destination together – which is fellowship and communion with God.

Reflection

❖ Give examples on how we as the team can lead the congregation into worship, and how we can create an atmosphere of worship for all.

Styles of Worship

36

Horizontal Axis vs. Vertical Axis of Worship

I lift up my eyes to you, to you who sit enthroned in heaven.
Psalm 123:1
Read Ezra 8:1–6

There are two axes when it comes to worship – the vertical and the horizontal axis.[18] The vertical axis is the space that represents our connection with God. By lifting hands in praise to Him, we focus on heaven and His presence. Even though God is omnipresent, this axis can represent us looking up to Him, and His Spirit coming down to us. When we truly worship, we can feel His comforting presence around us, and communion with Him in an intimate way.

The horizontal axis is symbolic for the worshipers. This is where we can be a part of the worship together as one body, and we see and experience each other praising. Another horizontal axis can be with the stage or pulpit. Here we can focus on the preacher and the Word. Depending on the positioning, we can also focus on the choir and worship team in this axis. We can experience this visual axis by seeing the pulpit, preacher, and worship team, as well as each other. This can also be an auditory axis where we hear the sound from the speakers and the congregation singing and worshiping. We break bread together (Holy Communion) and share in each other's testimonies. Communion is an amazing way both axes can be appreciated. We receive the wine and bread and look up to heaven and remember the sacrifice of Jesus, all while we experience this time of remembrance together as one body.

The reason we should be aware of these axes is to avoid any inappropriate use of these spaces. The vertical axis can be a cause of distractions or diversions when worshipers are tempted to focus on things like distractive lights, architecture, or art. Horizontal worship can be misused when the audience focuses on the worship team, and the worship team focuses on the responses of the audience. The worship team must be aware of the congregation, but their focus should be on God. Likewise, we should avoid any reasons why the congregations would focus on us on stage instead of toward heaven.

Reflection

- ❖ Do we have freedom to explore the different axes as we worship? Why or why not?
- ❖ How can we make sure the focus is on God and not on us?

37

Traditional vs. Contemporary Worship

Let the message of Christ dwell among you richly as you teach and admonish one another with all wisdom through psalms, hymns, and songs from the Spirit, singing to God with gratitude in your hearts.
Colossians 3:16
Read Acts 10 and 15:1–21

Ephesians 5:19 and Colossians 3:16 say that we should "sing psalms, hymns, and spiritual songs." Psalms can be scriptural songs, or songs found in the Word, that can be sung or recited with the congregation. Hymns are those songs with heartfelt meaning and prayerful language. Spiritual songs are those songs led by the spirit, where the worshiper can focus on God and sing and praise with his/her spirit.

There are many new contemporary Christian songs that have been released over the years. Many of them have powerful lyrics with wonderful melodies and accompanying music. These songs may speak to the current generation. However, every generation has their music that they have grown up with and associate with. There are songs that speak to every generation. As worship leaders, we must take extra care not to isolate any generation when we select our music and songs. We must be able to include all generations in our worship. To engage a younger generation, we could modernize old hymns. To engage an older generation we could sing contemporary songs with melodies and choruses that are easy to learn and follow.

The songs, music, and lyrics of traditional and contemporary worship will become challenged with every new generation. "We cannot follow the hits of today or great music of the past and think we have material that pleases God. We must be critical of the lyric content of our songs."[19] "He wants us to sing Scripture. He wants us to sing prayerful songs and songs of invisible power."[19]

During the establishment of the church after Jesus rose from the dead, the disciples converted many Jews, and they became the first church. An issue arose however when the Gentiles were also being converted, which led to dissension in the church. God gave Peter the answer to this in a dream in Acts 10:9–16. Paul also said in Romans 10:12 "For there is no difference between Jew and Gentile, the same Lord is Lord of all".

Ephesians 2:14 says that Jesus "has made the two one and has destroyed the barrier, the dividing wall of hostility". We need to ensure that we do not create a divide in our congregation with the songs that we sing to worship our God.

Reflection

- ❖ List some older hymns that you grew up with and that have meaningful lyrics. How can you make them more contemporary?
- ❖ List some newer songs you would like to introduce to the church. Will these songs allow all generations to worship with you?

The Role of the Worship Team

38

Dedication — Are We Willing?

Set your minds on things above, not earthly things.
Colossians 3:2
Read Exodus 35 and 36:1–7

The Greek word used for "mind" is **phroneo**, which means mind, sentiment, understanding, or opinion. The King James Version says affection. When we commit our mind and talent to something, it should have our full concentration and dedication. Our thoughts are engaged with the things we are passionate or sentimental about. These have meaning to us. Paul is asking us to set our minds to Godly things and to be passionate about them. Remember that Paul instructs us in Colossians 3:23 that "Whatever you do, work at it with all your heart, as working for the Lord, not for men."

In Exodus 31 we see two Israelites, Bezalel and Oholiab, who were filled with the Spirit of God and blessed with skill for arts and crafts. They had a special role in the construction of Moses' Tabernacle (see week 18). Exodus 36:2 says, "Then Moses summoned Bezalel and Oholiab and every skilled person to whom the Lord had given ability and **who was willing** to come and do the work." In Exodus 35, we read about all those who not only had the skill that God blessed them with, but was willing to use it for the glory of God. We also see that the people were dedicated in their crafts, and they wanted to ensure that they did their best. God has blessed us in so many ways, and He has given each of us a unique set of skills. How we choose to use those skills and talents depends on us. Are we willing to use what God has given us for His divine purpose?

Reflection

❖ What are you skilled at? What are you passionate about?
❖ How can you use these for God's kingdom?

39

Don't Be A Distraction

Let us throw off everything that hinders and
the sin that so easily entangles...
fixing our eyes on Jesus, the pioneer and perfector of faith.
Hebrews 12:1–2

The primary responsibility of the worship team is to focus on God and to help lead the congregation into worship. Sometimes, unfortunately, we can become a distraction to this process. Although obvious examples like glaring mistakes (wrong chords, timing, instruments not in tune) and unprofessional behavior on stage (talking, laughing, distracting gestures) come to mind, other things can be distracting to the worshiper as well. There may be a setting when loud music may be appropriate, like at concerts or rallies, but intentionally loud music during the service/ worship can turn the focus away from God and towards the music. Over enthusiastic instrumental solos (guitar, drum) detract from the lyrics and worship, and it may force the worshiper to observe this musical interlude. Certain lights and lighting can also have a distracting impact. A dark setting with spotlights on the stage can make the worship team the focal point, while overly bright settings may inhibit a worshiper from fully engaging in worship in fear of others watching. Key changes from song to song, causing long pauses, can also bring about unnecessary attention to the music or lack thereof. Picking similar keys and chord structures and rehearsing transitions can ensure a smoother flow to the set.

Know your craft by practicing on your own. This will limit any errors or mistakes and assist in fine-tuning your sound. The sound/ lighting / technical team should be prepared by knowing the set and order of service beforehand so that there are no errors or issues. The congregation may observe hand signals that are meant for communication within the team. The art of subtle gestures comes with practice. Whether all of these are intentional or unintentional, the spotlight can turn to us. We must ensure that the congregation stays focused on worship. By practicing our craft and preparing ourselves spiritually through prayer, we can become more observant and identify avoidable issues. We must try our best not to cause any distractions for the congregation as they worship and concentrate on God.

We should also avoid becoming distracted ourselves. In week 30, we saw how Peter was distracted by the waves and storm, and he started to sink into the water. But when he focused on Jesus he was saved. Psalm 119:15 (ESV) says, "I will meditate on your precepts and **fix my eyes** on your ways." We should do our best to concentrate on Jesus, even while we are playing or singing, because our ultimate goal is to worship together.

<u>Reflection</u>

❖ What are some possible distractions occurring with your worship team?

❖ How can you alleviate this?

40

Be Aware of Your Audience

There before me was a great multitude that no one could
count, from every nation, tribe, people and language,
standing before the throne and before the Lamb.
Revelation 7:9
Read Galatians 2:11–21

Many churches are made up of multigenerational congregants, and others may have multicultural worshipers. A challenge many ethnic, multicultural, and multigenerational churches face is how to engage all congregants in worship, regardless of age, language, or cultural differences. Is this possible? The worship team has a difficult job of balancing the specific preferences of each group. All groups must be taken into consideration when choosing songs for worship. By not considering a group, you could possibly exclude members from participating in worship. This doesn't mean that we must manipulate the service to reach certain groups. We must learn to be flexible. If there is a mix of generations, we can incorporate both old and new songs. If it is multicultural, we can select songs that speak to all groups. It would also help if these groups were represented within our teams.

The groups that make up the church become an

important determinant for the worshiping style of the church. Of course there are different styles and preferences among various ethnicities and cultures. We must take care, however, not to fall into our own form of **ethnocentrism** – the belief that one's own culture is superior to another. In week 7 we discussed Heavenly worship. In Heaven, all races and cultures will worship our God together, as one voice.

In week 37, we were reminded that Ephesians 2:14 says that Jesus "has made the two groups one and has destroyed the barrier, the dividing wall of hostility". We discussed the importance of being inclusive to all generations. We studied that Peter saw a vision from God and why the Gentiles were meant to be part of the future church. However, we read in Galatians 2:11–14 that Peter separated himself from dining with the Gentiles. Paul chastises Peter for this hypocrisy. We must remember that we are the Body of Christ and we worship as one. It is the responsibility of the worship team to do their part to ensure this happens.

Reflection

❖ Identify the various groups in your church.
❖ Give examples of how you can include all groups in your worship.

41

Recognize the Move of the Spirit

But the Advocate, the Holy Spirit, whom
the Father will send in my name,
will teach you all things and will remind
you of everything I have said to you.
John 14:26
Read Acts 4:23–31 and 10:44–48

Throughout the book of Acts, we read about the power of the Holy Spirit on the disciples and new believers. In both Acts 4 and 10, we see that the believers were in an attitude of worship, prayer, and receiving the Word. The Holy Spirit moved when the people of God were anxiously seeking Him.

Today when we worship, we must be aware of the same move of the Holy Spirit. When the heart of the congregation is seeking the will of God and truly worshiping in adoration, the Holy Spirit's presence can be felt. This is when the worship team must learn to be submissive to the presence of God. Even if we have a planned order of worship, if the Holy Spirit is engaging the people, then we cannot hinder that.

This does not mean that worship should be unorganized or unstructured. For the most part, a planned structure needs to be followed. However, if the Spirit is leading people into worship, and we observe this response, then we need to learn to be obedient to the Spirit. For example, if the congregation is responding to the bridge of a song, then we should have the freedom to repeat it, even though it wasn't what was practiced during rehearsal. This is the responsibility of the worship leader to recognize the response of the congregation, and to signal the team for any changes.

Proper signals and communication can alleviate any uncertainty of the progression of the song. If the team has spent time in prayer and devotion, the Spirit may even lead to change songs right before or during the set. Understandably, this can make any music team shudder. But this comes with practice so that all the team members, leaders, vocalists, and musicians, are comfortable with any on-stage adjustments or changes. When we follow the leading of the Holy Spirit, we will see that the whole service will come together and revolve around Him.

Reflection

❖ How can we be aware of the congregation's responses and worship?
❖ What are some examples of how we adjust our sets accordingly?

42

Song Selection and Themes

Sing to the Lord a new song; Sing to the Lord, all the earth.
Sing to the Lord, praise his name; Proclaim
his salvation day after day.
Psalm 96:1–2
Read Psalm 96

A vital responsibility of the team is the song selection process. This can be challenging, as everyone has differing tastes and preferences. During this selection, the team should consider songs with meaning and not just based on the latest and most "popular" songs. Songs should teach about the nature and character of God, about His love, and Jesus' sacrifice. The lyrics should engage the worshiper and reflect on spiritual things. Singing new songs gives an opportunity to expand our song list. We should be careful that we are not introducing too many new songs simultaneously. Then the focus of the worshiper will be on trying to learn the song instead of on God. Songs that have repetitive lyrics can be powerful, but the team must take caution that it does not become chant-like or too repetitious. Speaking to the pastor or minister of the Word prior to the selection can also help identify common themes.

Songs selected in prayer will have a theme or connection throughout the service. It is common to hear about prayerfully selected songs having common themes with the preacher's message, even without prior consultation. We cannot limit God. If there is a message that the Spirit is giving to the church, and the church is receptive, then it will be apparent. When God is speaking to the church, a connection to the theme will be present. Song lyrics become applicable to the message. It may even speak to individuals on a personal level. All this can be experienced as the team (and the ministers) spends more time in prayer and devotion.

We don't need to force a theme for every service, but having themes can allow thoughtful choosing of songs and avoid any arbitrary or random selection. Some themes can include:

1) God's Greatness and Awe
2) God's Glory
3) The Kingdom of God
4) Jesus Savior/ Redeemer
5) Jesus Sacrifice/ Blood of Christ /Forgiveness of Sins
6) The Love of Christ
7) The Power of the Spirit
   • Healing
   • Strength/ Overcoming Difficulties

Psalm 96:8 (NKJV) says "give to the Lord the glory due His name." As worship leaders, our songs need to glorify God and allow the congregation to worship Him. If the songs we select divert from this, then we are not doing our jobs. The songs we sing should encourage the congregation to worship freely. Selecting songs with meaningful lyrics and that are not difficult to sing can give the worshiper an opportunity to focus on God and have deeper connection with Him.

<u>Reflection</u>

- ❖ What are some themes you have used in the past?
- ❖ What themes could you use for future services?
- ❖ Have you witnessed worship themes and other parts of the service coinciding?

43

Team Dynamic & Team Building

Therefore encourage one another and build each other up...
1 Thessalonians 5:11
Read Ecclesiastes 4:9–12

In the book of Romans, Paul instructs us to grow together and encourage each other. "May the God who gives endurance and encouragement give you the same attitude of mind toward each other that Christ Jesus had, so that with one mind and one voice you may glorify the God and Father of our Lord Jesus Christ" Romans 15:5–6. Solomon, in all his wisdom, also understood the importance of teamwork and working together to achieve a goal. In Ecclesiastes 4, he tells us "two are better than one, because they have good return for their labor" (v.9) and that "a cord of three strands is not quickly broken" (v.12).

We must not be afraid to encourage each other. Criticism is not taken well by anyone; but brotherly/ sisterly advice can be invaluable. This however comes from a place of humility from both parties. The person correcting must come with a humble attitude and the one being corrected must be willing to be advised. "Biblical confrontation comes from the position of an ally, working with Christian brothers and sisters to help them stand against a human tendency to sin."[20]

As the worship team, we have one common goal—which is to present our best worship to the Lord. When we worship together, the congregation will worship with us. If we are in discord, it will become apparent to the church. We are allowed to have artistic differences. This diversity is what makes us unique in the body of Christ (remember week 10). But we should be encouraged by each other so that we can not only grow in our crafts, but to ensure that the best worship is offered with the congregation and ultimately to God.

Reflection

* ❖ As a leader, how can you approach a team member to correct, and encourage and advise him/her?
* ❖ As team members, how can you encourage each other?
* ❖ How do you address concerns with your leaders?

44

Mentor/ Mentee Relationship

Dear brothers and sisters, pattern your lives after mine,
and learn from those who follow our example.
Philippians 3:17 (NLT)
Read 1 Timothy 4

One example in the New Testament of a mentor/ mentee relationship is that of the apostle Paul and Timothy. Timothy was young and may have had a timid personality. Paul considered himself as his mentor, teacher, and spiritual father ("son in the faith" 1 Timothy 1:2). Throughout the letters to Timothy, Paul advised the young apostle in many areas.

Paul tells Timothy to "train yourself" (1 Timothy 4:7) and to be confident. He advises him to "set an example in speech, in conduct, in love, in faith, and in purity (1 Timothy 4:12). He teaches how to treat the elderly and younger brothers and sisters, as well as widows in 1 Timothy 5. He tells Timothy to conduct all things in fairness and kindness. Paul advises us that as Christians we have the Spirit of power, love, and self-discipline, not of timidity. He warns us to "watch your life and doctrine" (4:16). He also warns against financial temptations, the evil desires of youth, pointless arguments, and gossip (godless chatter) in 2 Timothy 2:16. Finally, Paul gives Timothy the authority to "preach the word...correct, rebuke and encourage" (2 Timothy 4:2).

As a worship team, we must always be looking to improve. In 1 Timothy 4:14, Paul advises us to "not neglect your gift". The gift of our talents that God has bestowed upon us was given to us for a purpose, which is to utilize them to glorify His kingdom. We can do this by growing our talents, instead of sitting idle and being satisfied in our current state. By seeking the advice of a mentor, whether it is musical or spiritual, it will enhance your growth. This could include someone on the pastoral staff, ministry leader or elder, band member, or even a friend in faith that you look up to. You should also consider mentoring new team members and even those that are newer in faith.

<u>Reflection</u>

❖ Think about your mentors. How can they help you grow?

❖ How can you mentor someone on the team?

45

Pursuit of Perfection

"You therefore must be perfect, as your
heavenly Father is perfect.
Matthew 5:48 (ESV)

The pursuit of perfection is a challenge many artists struggle with. Whether it is in our talent to play an instrument, vocal abilities, or other function, we strive for musical and technical perfection. This is an admirable trait. This pursuit however should never impede the pursuit of the Holy Spirit. We must take care that it does not cross over to perfectionism. "Perfectionists set absolute and usually quite arbitrary standards by which to judge themselves and others. Their standards may be so high that the result is a paralyzing inactivity. On the other hand, those who are content to pursue excellence are unafraid to scale the heights. For them the chief issue is improvement."[20] We should take care not to confuse the pursuit of perfection with the pursuit of excellence. We should all strive to excel.

We aren't supposed to be perfect. We must make sure that we first strive for true worship in Spirit and Truth, even if there are imperfections in the music and singing. To improve, we can listen to recordings of our worship or rehearsals to critique ourselves. But the true test is to gauge the level of worship of the people, as well as our own worship during the service. Remember, God is looking at our hearts during the worship, not how flawlessly we sang, played instruments, or performed our service duties. It is up to us to find a balance between seeking excellence and seeking God through our worship.

We must also take care not to compare our gifts to others' gifts. "Each one should test their own actions. Then they can take pride in themselves alone, without comparing themselves to someone else, for each one should carry their own load" Galatians 6:4.

Reflection

- ❖ When does perfectionism become inhibiting to worship?
- ❖ How can we strive for excellence without compromising the move of the Holy Spirit?

Outcomes & Effects of Worship

46

Power of Worship

But you shall receive power when the
Holy Spirit has come upon you;
and you shall be witnesses to me in Jerusalem,
and… to the end of the earth.
Acts 1:8 (NKJV)

We offer our worship and praises to God because of our pure adoration for Him. But something else that can occur during our worship is the powerful move of the Holy Spirit. The Bible offers us many examples of when the power of God became evident while His people worshiped.

In week 6, we learned that King Solomon was dedicating the temple he had built for God's presence, and in accordance to the arrangements of his father David (1 Chron. 28:13), the musicians and singers (Levites) were to play in unison as with one voice. As they raised their voices and sang with the instruments, God's holy presence filled the temple. "All the Levites who were musicians…stood on the east side of the altar, dressed in fine linen and playing cymbals, harps and lyres. They were accompanied by 120 priests sounding trumpets." "Then the temple of the Lord was filled with the cloud, **and the priests could not perform their service** because of the cloud, for the glory of the Lord filled the temple of God (2 Chronicles 5:12–14).

In week 23, we discussed 2 Chronicles 20, where the Lord told Jehoshaphat that the battle was not his to fight, but that God would defeat the enemy. In fact, God said in verse 17, "You will not have to fight this battle. Take up your positions; stand firm and **see the deliverance** the LORD will give you." He told Jehoshaphat to stand back and watch His power take control of their situation.

In week 31, we read that Paul and Silas were freed from prison through their prayer and singing of hymns (Acts 16). Through their worship, the power of God came upon that place. There was a violent earthquake, the foundations were shaken and their chains fell off. Besides the physical manifestations, the jailer and his family were also saved.

In week 26, we read about Joshua and the Israelite army. In Joshua 6:4–5, the Lord said to Joshua, "Have seven priests carry trumpets of rams' horns in front of the ark. On the seventh day, march around the city seven times, with the priests blowing the trumpets. When you hear them sound a long blast on the trumpets, have the whole army give a loud shout; then **the wall of the city will collapse** and the army will go up, everyone straight in." The combination of the sound of the trumpets, followed by shouts from the army was the signal for God to destroy the walls of Jericho. The power of the Holy Spirit is evident even today, and every worshiper must seek it.

<u>Reflection</u>

❖ As worshipers, how will you know if the power of God is in your worship and church? Discuss examples.

47

Healing

Heal me, O LORD, and I shall be healed; Save me,
and I shall be saved, For You are my praise.
Jeremiah 17:14 (NKJV)
Read Luke 8:40–48

There is healing through our worship. When we sit in the presence of God, the power of the Holy Spirit can heal us, not just physically, but spiritually, mentally and emotionally. In Luke 8 we read about a woman with an illness for 12 years, and when she touched Jesus she was immediately healed. Then she bowed down, trembling, and worshiped Him. "Now when the woman saw that she was not hidden, she came trembling; and falling down before Him, she declared to Him in the presence of all the people the reason she had touched Him and how she was healed immediately" (Luke 8:47 NKJV). She knew that if she went to Jesus and touched Him, she would be healed. This wasn't a hunch or speculation on her part. She knew that there was healing power in Jesus. Just a few chapters before in Luke 6:19, the people were touching Jesus to be healed, "because power was coming from him and healing them all." They came to Him, and they were healed. When we come to worship God, we are healed because of His presence.

"Worship not only brings healing to our life issues, it also empowers us to face the realities of our life in the world with the conviction that the last word is not the death evil brings, but the resurrection Jesus gives. When we are healed and empowered by worship, our day-to-day lives at home, at work, and at leisure take on a new dimension."[21] Jesus can bring physical healing, but He heals our spirits and our mental being as well. God set us free from the bondage of sin through His Son Jesus Christ, so that our spirit can have communion with the Spirit of God. This communion, which we enjoy through prayer and worship, heals our spirit. "He heals the brokenhearted and binds up their wounds" (Psalm 147:3).

Reflection

❖ Which areas of your life can true heartfelt worship heal?
❖ How can your worship (private or corporate) result in healing?

48

Preparation for Receiving the Word

But the seed falling on good soil refers to someone
who hears the word and understands it.
This is the one who produces a crop, yielding a
hundred, sixty or thirty times what was sown.
Mathew 13:23
Read Mathew 13:1–23

Worship is a vital component of any service, and it should not be viewed as a precursor to other upcoming parts of a service. But it can lead the worshipers to be more open to receive the Word/ message. In Exodus 15–17, we read about Moses and the Israelites' struggles through the desert. They were not willing to follow the ways of God. This led them to become disobedient and, as a result, their hearts became hardened. Today, through life's hardships, trials and tests, disappointments, and even pride, our hearts can become hardened. When our hearts are hardened, then it becomes difficult to hear God and align with His will in our lives. Pure worship, however, can melt even the most hardened heart.

Worship can be like the water that softens the soil before planting seeds. In the parable of the different soils in

Mathew 13, Jesus teaches about seeds planted in different types of soils. The good soil is representative of a person that hears the Word, understands and accepts it, and keeps it in their heart. It will strengthen them during difficult times. If we have hardened hearts, then when we hear the Word we will not be reminded of it during times of trouble—like the seeds that fell on rocky ground. Worship can bring us closer to God and soften our hearts, so that when we hear the Word it will speak to us and be kept in our hearts and minds.

<u>Reflection</u>

❖ Why is it important to select songs that may be meaningful to the worshiper?
❖ How important is the worship parts of the service compared to other parts?

49

Worship as Evangelism

They broke bread in their homes and ate
together with glad and sincere hearts,
praising God and enjoying the favor of all the
people. And the Lord added to their number
daily those who were being saved.
Acts 2:46–47
Read Acts 2

Worship is so powerful that it speaks to people. It speaks to the believer, and gives them strength and hope. It can also touch the unbeliever, because they can sense a different and spiritual environment.

On the day of Pentecost in Acts 2, we see the Holy Spirit coming down on the apostles while they gathered and worshiped. They began to speak in different languages and the surrounding people started to crowd around them in amazement. After Peter had given his message about Jesus, "Those who accepted his message were baptized, and about three thousand were added to their number that day" (v. 41).

There are many ways to evangelize to people. Some may prefer an intellectual conversation. Some may need a listening ear and prayer. But many people are touched by song and music. In week 22, we discussed the impact of music on people. This is why many of us are drawn to music concerts, live performances, or even stop to listen to a street performer or subway musician. Worship can touch people also. When we worship in the presence of non-believers, we hope and pray that the words and music can speak to them. As long as they come with an open mind and heart, God will stir something inside. So it is vital that our worship comes from a place of sincerity and not for show. When our worship becomes a performance, then it can seem no different to a non-believer than attending a secular concert.

Although our worship is a source of evangelism, we must ensure that it is not the end goal or only purpose. "Good worship will be evangelistic, but that is not its primary purpose, for it is directed toward God, not toward the neighbor. No passage in Scripture says, 'worship the Lord to attract the unbeliever'. Rather in countless texts we are commanded, invited, urged, wooed to worship the trinity because God is worthy of our praise."[22] "The church is first a worshiping community. Evangelism and other functions ministry flow from the worship of the church."[23]

Reflection

* Do you use worship as a tool to grow your church, or to show Jesus' love and grow his kingdom?
* How can your worship change an unbeliever?

50

Unity/ As One

"I pray ...that all of them may be one" John 17:20–21
"that they may be brought to complete unity" John 17:23
Read John 17:14–25

In John 17 Jesus prayed for his disciples and for future believers. He prayed that Christians would be unified together, work together, believe together, and spread the Good News together. The early church understood this. Acts 4:32 tells us that "all the believers were one in heart and mind."

Koinonia is the Greek word for communion, fellowship, and to participate. In Acts 2:44, we see that "all the believers were together and had everything in common." They strengthened and encouraged each other. They broke bread and praised God together, and they grew in number. We must realize that we have a unified goal in the ministry of the church and in worship. Under the guidance of the Holy Spirit and the leadership of the pastoral team, and with the understanding that each team member has a vital role within the church, we must try to work as one mind and in one accord.

In Week 10 we discussed the Body of Christ detailed

in 1 Corinthians 12. It says that we are one body with many parts, with each member having a particular function, but remaining part of the whole. Ephesians 4:16 reiterates this by reminding us that our whole body is supported by ligaments, and that all parts of the body function together as a whole. Just as all the parts of our body must function for the good of the whole, so must the church and all of its member's function cohesively and efficiently, for the benefit of the church.

Reflection

- ❖ What are the different roles in your church and during your service?
- ❖ How can we ensure that we all work together and be united to glorify God?

Supplemental Devotionals—
Special Services/ Holy Days

51

Resurrection Sunday

While he was blessing them, he left them
and was taken up into heaven.
Then they worshiped him and returned
to Jerusalem with great joy.
Luke 24:51–52
Read Luke 24

Easter is a time of celebrating the victory of Jesus defeating death and saving us from sin. During this time, we are also inundated with images of colorful eggs, chocolate, and the Easter Bunny. It is important that we as Christians are not distracted by this depiction of the ultimate sacrifice made by our Lord and Savior. We should be reminded during this time what He paid on that cross so that we can be freed from sin and be reunited with the Father.

When we read Luke 24, we witness the amazing interaction Jesus had with his followers after he rose from the dead. On the road to Emmaus, we see Jesus walking with two believers. They, however, did not recognize Him. But their eyes were opened when He broke bread with them (v.31). Later we see Jesus was with the disciples, and "he opened their minds so they could understand the scriptures" (v.45). Sometimes we go through life and get caught up in the monotony of our routines. Without realizing we go on autopilot. Our eyes are closed because of routine. Other times we may be so busy we lose sight of our purpose. Our eyes are closed because we are distracted. The devil looks to deceive and close the eyes of people. 2 Corinthians 4:4 says, "the god of this age has blinded the eyes of the unbelievers, so that they cannot see they light of the gospel." Jesus opened the eyes of the disciples after His resurrection. We must pray that God opens our eyes to understand His Word and see His will for our lives.

As people come to the Easter service, we as worshipers should be able to remind them of what Jesus did. This is a very special time. The songs we sing should remind people of His sacrifice and victory over sin and death.

Reflection

- ❖ How can your service speak to those that only attend church during special services, like Easter?
- ❖ What can God open our eyes to everyday?

52

Christmas Week

Suddenly a great company of the heavenly host
appeared with the angel, praising God and saying,
"Glory to God in the highest heaven, and on earth
peace to those on whom his favor rests."
Luke 2:13–14
Read Mathew 2

To many people, both Christians and non-Christians, Christmas can be one of the best times of the year. People everywhere are excited for the holiday and spend time with family and friends. It is a season about giving and good will, and people are joyful, cheerful, and feel generous. This is a great time to minister to people about the true meaning of Christmas. There are many Christians that attend services only on holy or special days. Or there may be guests visiting local churches, curious to see what Christmas and Christianity is all about. Many will come expecting Christmas carols, plays, and other activities. Along with the message of Christ, this is an opportunity for people to hear God's Word through song, and to experience true heartfelt worship. The songs we sing should reveal the beauty of the gift of Christ, who left his heavenly throne to free us from sin.

Jesus is our atoning gift from God. This gift was freely given to us because of God's love for us. When Jesus was born on Earth, wise men brought gifts of gold, frankincense and myrrh. But what were the meanings of these gifts? They may have been customary things to give for very special occasions, but there is a deeper meaning. Gold was used in many materials in the building of the tabernacle of Moses and the Temple built by Solomon. It was used in the Ark of the Covenant (Exodus 37:1–7), in many articles within the tabernacle (Exodus 37:10–28), and within Solomon's Temple (2 Chron. 3:4–10; 4:7–8, 19–22). Gold has a holy as well as heavenly representation. Gold also symbolized royalty and was given as gifts for a king (1 Kings 10:2). Frankincense was used in the Old Testament as part of fragrant incense for worship to God (Exodus 30:34). It is also seen in Revelation representing the prayers of the saints (Revelation 5:8; 8:3–4). The priests were to burn the incense as part of their duties (Exodus 30:7–8; Luke 1:9). Incense represents prayer and worship. Myrrh had many purposes. We see many biblical examples of its use as anointing oil by the priests (Exodus 30:22–32) and to anoint the priests for consecration (Exodus 29:21). It was also used as preparation for burial and embalming (John 19:39) and to alleviate pain (Mark 15:23).

Based on these examples, we understand that the gifts to Jesus were prophetic in nature. Gold represents Jesus as our God and King; frankincense represents Jesus as our Priest; and myrrh represents the anointing of Jesus and preparation for His death. Pure worship can be seen as our gift and offerings to God. Just as the gifts from the wise men had purpose, our heartfelt worship is also very significant and meaningful!

<u>Reflection</u>

❖ What can you offer to God as your gift to Him?
❖ How can your gift help others around you?

Conclusion

The role of the worship team is vital. It is not just about playing music or singing songs that make us feel good. Worship is not another part of the service for congregants to enjoy, or for some, sit through. Worship is a way of life—giving glory and adoration to our heavenly Father. When worship becomes more about the song selection, musicianship, and production, then we've lost the opportunity for a very meaningful connection with God. Additionally, worship should not be limited to a scheduled time on specified days. We should be in a state of worship at all times. "Our concept of worship must expand beyond an activity that somehow starts and stops."[24]

Throughout this year, you have discussed with your team important things like:

1) Who do we worship?
2) How can we express our worship?
3) Who are some biblical examples we can learn from and emulate?
4) How do we lead with the guidance of the Holy Spirit?
5) What is our function and purpose on the team?
6) What does our worship achieve?

These and other questions—along with your dialogue—should have helped you understand the importance of your gift and role on the team and in the church. There are many other areas and other examples of worship that can be studied and discussed by the worship team. This devotional has prayerfully touched upon some vital topics so that the team may be encouraged and strengthened, and to fully grow in the Lord and know His complete will. By studying and discussing the applications of these topics, my hope is that you have grown spiritually and faithfully as a team.

As we end, reflect back on what you have learned through this devotional. Have you grown in your knowledge of God and worship? Have you connected more closely with God? I pray that the answers to this are a resounding "Yes!" I challenge the team to go back and delve deeper into some devotionals that engaged you and the team the most. I hope that these topics will lead you into further research of worship and discover a deeper relationship with God.

End Notes

1. Roxanne Brant, *Ministering to the Lord* (New Kensington, PA: Whitaker House, 1987), 14

2. Stephen R. Phifer, *Worship That Pleases God* (Victoria, BC, Canada: Trafford Publishing, 2005), 42

3. Christian Assemblies International, *The Music of Johann Sebastian Bach.* Available from: https://www.cai.org/bible-studies/music-johann-sebastian-bach

4. Robert E. Webber, *The Complete Library of Christian Worship, Vol. III* (Peabody, MA: Hendrickson Publishers, Inc., 1993), 364

5. Andrew E. Hill, *Enter His Courts with Praise* (Nashville: Star Song Publishing Group, 1993), 156

6. Dallas Willard, *The Spirit of the Disciplines* (New York: HarperCollins Publishers, 1988), 7

7. Dallas Willard, *The Spirit of the Disciplines* (New York: HarperCollins Publishers, 1988), 164

8. Dallas Willard, *The Spirit of the Disciplines* (New York: HarperCollins Publishers, 1988), 176

9. Dallas Willard, *The Spirit of the Disciplines* (New York: HarperCollins Publishers, 1988), 138

10. Dallas Willard, *The Spirit of the Disciplines* (New York: HarperCollins Publishers, 1988), 143–144

11. Stephen R. Phifer, *Worship That Pleases God* (Victoria, BC, Canada: Trafford Publishing, 2005), 76

12. Simon Chan, Simon, *Pentecostal Theology and the Christian Spiritual Tradition* (Eugene, OR: Wipf and Stock Publishers, 2000), 66

13. Robert E. Webber, *The Divine Embrace* (Grand Rapids, MI: Baker Books, 2008), 94

14. Robert E. Webber, *The Divine Embrace* (Grand Rapids, MI: Baker Books, 2008), 95

15. James F. White, *Introduction to Christian Worship* (Nashville: Abingdon Press, 1980), 112

16. Andrew E. Hill, *Enter His Courts with Praise* (Nashville: Star Song Publishing Group, 1993), 113

17. Stephen R. Phifer, *Worship That Pleases God* (Victoria, BC, Canada: Trafford Publishing, 2005), 92–102

18. James F. White, *Introduction to Christian Worship* (Nashville: Abingdon Press, 1980), 85

19. Stephen R. Phifer, *Worship That Pleases God* (Victoria, BC, Canada: Trafford Publishing, 2005), 167

20. Robert E. Webber, *The Complete Library of Christian Worship, Vol. III* (Peabody, MA: Hendrickson Publishers, Inc., 1993), 384

21. Robert E. Webber, *Worship is a Verb* (Peabody, MA: Hendrickson Publishers, 2004), 205

22. Marva J. Dawn, *A Royal Waste of Time* (Grand Rapids, MI: Wm. B. Eerdmans Publishing Co, 1999), 123

23. Robert E. Webber, *Worship is a Verb* (Peabody, MA: Hendrickson Publishers, 2004), 8

24. Stephen R. Phifer, *Worship That Pleases God* (Victoria, BC, Canada: Trafford Publishing, 2005), 85

Bibliography

Brant, Roxanne. *Ministering to the Lord*. New Kensington, PA: Whitaker House, 1987

Chan, Simon. *Pentecostal Theology and the Christian Spiritual Tradition*. Eugene, OR: Wipf and Stock Publishers, 2000

Christian Assemblies International. *The Music of Johann Sebastian Bach*. Available from:

https://www.cai.org/bible-studies/music-johann-sebastian-bach

Dawn, Marva J. *A Royal Waste of Time*. Grand Rapids, MI: Wm. B. Eerdmans Publishing Co, 1999

Hill, Andrew E. *Enter His Courts with Praise*. Nashville: Star Song Publishing Group, 1993

Phifer, Stephen R. *Worship That Pleases God*. Victoria, BC, Canada: Trafford Publishing, 2005

Webber, Robert E. *The Complete Library of Christian Worship, Vol. III*. Peabody, MA: Hendrickson Publishers, Inc., 1993

Webber, Robert E. *The Divine Embrace*. Grand Rapids, MI: Baker Books, 2008

Webber, Robert E. *Worship is a Verb*. Peabody, MA: Hendrickson Publishers, 2004

White, James F. *Introduction to Christian Worship*. Nashville: Abingdon Press, 1980

Willard, Dallas. *The Spirit of the Disciplines*. New York: HarperCollins Publishers, 1988

Notes:

Notes:

Notes:

Notes:

Printed in the United States
By Bookmasters